breakfasts

breakfasts

Jacque Malouf

photography by Tara Fisher

conran
OCTOPUS

Drinks

Rosewater and mint-scented lemonade

Serves 4
Preparation time: 30 minutes

90 g/3 oz caster sugar
4 large leafy mint sprigs, plus extra for serving
a handful of ice cubes
240 ml/8 fl oz lemon juice (the juice of about
   6 large lemons)
2 teaspoons rosewater, or to taste

This thirst quenching rose- and mint-scented lemonade is worlds apart from the commercially produced stuff. There is just enough sweetness to tame the sharp lemon juice without the drink being overly sugary.

Rosewater is available from Middle Eastern grocers, some supermarkets and health food stores. As it varies in strength from brand to brand it is best to add it in small amounts and taste as you go. You can also place a few of the squeezed lemon halves in the bottom of the jug, if desired.

Place the sugar and mint sprigs in a small pan with 6 tablespoons water. Set over a low heat and stir until the sugar dissolves. Turn up the heat and allow the water to bubble for a few minutes until it becomes a light syrup. Set aside to cool.

When the syrup is cool discard the mint and pour it into a large serving jug with the ice cubes. Add the lemon juice and 500 ml/18 fl oz cold water and stir to combine. Add the rosewater to taste then top with the remaining mint sprigs and serve straight away.

Minty mango lassi

Serves 2
Preparation time: 5 minutes

200 g/7 oz very ripe mango flesh, cubed
250 g/9 oz yoghurt
2 teaspoons caster sugar
2 large mint leaves
8 ice cubes
a few sprigs of mint, to serve

The mint and mango in this fragrant, cooling drink act as a subtle refreshing element rather than a dominant fruitiness.

Make sure you use a nicely perfumed, sweet ripe mango, such as the Alphonso variety.

Place the mango, yoghurt, sugar, mint and ice cubes into a blender and whizz until smooth and thick. You can add a little cold water if you prefer a drink that's a bit thinner.

Pour the lassi into 2 chilled glasses, garnish with the mint sprigs and serve immediately.

Watermelon and strawberry juice

Serves 2
Preparation time: 5 minutes

400 g/14 oz watermelon flesh, cubed and seeds removed
150 g/5 oz strawberries, washed and hulled
ice cubes, to serve

This refreshing summer juice should be made with the sweetest fruit possible.

For a zingy kick serve with some fruity ice cubes. To make these, place some chunks of fruit, whole mint leaves or small lime wedges into the ice cube tray before filling with water and freezing.

Feed the watermelon cubes and strawberries through a juicer and divide between 2 chilled glasses. Stir before drinking and serve with ice cubes.

Pink grapefruit, orange and lime juice

Serves 2
Preparation time: 5 minutes

2 pink or ruby grapefruits, chilled
4 large oranges, chilled
a few dashes of lime juice
2 lime wedges for serving

The tartness of grapefruit and lime makes this blended juice an invigorating wake up call. You can add a little more orange juice if you prefer it sweeter.

Squeeze the grapefruits and oranges, discarding the seeds. Place the juice in a jug and add a dash or two of lime juice to taste – only add a tiny bit if the grapefruit is rather tart. Stir well, pour into 2 chilled glasses and serve with the lime wedges.

White hot chocolate with cinnamon, cardamom and vanilla

Serves 4
Preparation time: 10 minutes

800 ml/1 pint 8oz milk
large pinch ground cinnamon
large pinch ground cardamom
few drops of vanilla extract
120 g/4 oz best quality white chocolate, finely chopped
4 cinnamon sticks, to serve

This is hot chocolate with a twist – a velvety smooth concoction of white chocolate and milk with a hint of fragrant spices.

Place the milk in a pan set over a medium heat. Stir in the cinnamon, cardamom and vanilla. Bring up to the boil then take the pan off the heat. Add the chopped chocolate and stir until melted. Taste and adjust the spices if necessary.

Pour the spiced hot chocolate into 4 heatproof serving cups and place a cinnamon stick in each as a stirrer.

Pomegranate and orange juice with orange blossom water

Serves 2
Preparation time: 15 minutes

1 large pomegranate
4 large oranges, chilled
1 teaspoon orange blossom water
ice cubes, to serve

Although the pomegranate seeds are a little fiddly to remove, it is well worth it for this unusual and exotically perfumed drink.

Orange blossom (or orange flower) water is available from Middle Eastern grocers, some supermarkets and health food stores.

Cut the pomegranate in half and remove the seeds with your fingers, avoiding the yellow pith, which is rather bitter. Keep the seeds to one side and discard the rest of the pomegranate.

Squeeze the oranges, discarding any seeds and place in a blender with the pomegranate seeds and orange blossom water. Whizz the ingredients together then strain and serve in chilled glasses with a handful of ice cubes.

Butternut squash and stem ginger smoothie

Serves 2
Preparation time: 30 minutes,
including cooking and cooling the squash

150 g/5 oz peeled cooked butternut squash cubes
300 ml/11 fl oz milk
½ teaspoon finely chopped stem ginger
2 tablespoons stem ginger syrup
3 tablespoons ground almonds
2 heaped tablespoons thick yoghurt
large pinch mixed spice
ice cubes, to serve

Inspired by pumpkin pie, this odd-sounding drink is wonderfully spiced and surprisingly light.

Stem ginger is preserved knobs of ginger steeped in a sweet syrup and sold in jars. If you don't have any you can achieve a similarly sweet and spicy effect by using maple syrup instead, plus a few extra pinches of mixed spice.

Place all ingredients but the ice cubes into a blender and whizz until smooth.

Pour the smoothie into 2 chilled glasses with a few ice cubes and serve.

Raspberry and banana yoghurt smoothie

Serves 2
Preparation time: 5 minutes

60 g/2 oz raspberries
2 bananas, peeled and cut into chunks
1 tablespoon runny honey
300 g/11 oz yoghurt, chilled
200 ml/7 fl oz milk, chilled

Place all of the ingredients into a blender and whizz until smooth. Pour into 2 chilled glasses and serve.

Cereal

Macadamia, coconut and dried tropical fruit granola

Serves 6
Preparation time: 30 minutes

250 g/9 oz large, whole rolled oats
75 g/2½ oz desiccated coconut
90 g/3 oz macadamia nuts, halved or in large pieces
45 g/1½ oz hulled pumpkin seeds
120 ml/4 fl oz clear honey, warmed
30 g/1 oz dried unsweetened mango, chopped
30 g/1 oz dried unsweetened papaya, chopped
30 g/1 oz dried unsweetened pineapple
45 g/1½ oz banana chips, roughly chopped

This granola is full of great flavours and textures. You can adapt it to suit your taste. Large nuts, such as hazelnuts, almonds and Brazil nuts work well, and any combination of dried fruits will do the trick. Try to find plump fleshy dried fruit – not the leathery stuff sold in thin slices. Banana chips are crispy sweetened banana slices available from health food shops and some supermarkets

Preheat the oven to 180°C/350°F/gas mark 4. Place the oats, coconut, nuts, pumpkin seeds and honey in a large mixing bowl and stir in the honey to lightly coat the ingredients. Tip onto a large wide baking tray and spread the mixture in a thin layer. If your tray isn't large enough you can spread the mixture over 2 trays and swap them over halfway through cooking. Place in the oven for 16–20 minutes, stirring often until golden brown. Take out of the oven and allow to cool.

Transfer to a large mixing bowl and stir in the dried fruit and banana chips. Eat straight away or store in an airtight jar. Serve with icy cold milk or a dollop of thick yoghurt.

Blueberry, dried peach and pistachio muesli

Serves 4
Preparation time: 10 minutes plus 1 hour to soak the oats

150 g/5 oz jumbo oats
250 ml/9 fl oz clear apple juice
120 g/4 oz Greek yoghurt, plus extra to serve
1 crisp red apple, grated or finely chopped
60 g/2 oz dried peaches, chopped
15 g/½ oz pistachios, chopped
15 g/½ oz flaked almonds, toasted
75 g/2½ oz blueberries
clear honey, to serve

This very filling, wet muesli is full of flavour and crunch. The berries, nuts and dried fruits can be substituted with your favourites – but go easy on citrus fruits as they can curdle the yoghurt.

Place the oats and apple juice into a bowl, then stir, cover and leave in the fridge for at least an hour. You can leave it overnight if you prefer.

Add the yoghurt, most of the grated apple, dried peaches, nuts and berries and stir to mix well. Spoon into 4 serving bowls, and top with the remaining grated apple, dried peaches, nuts and berries. Lightly drizzle with honey and top with a dollop of Greek yoghurt.

Crunchy sesame granola

Serves 6
Preparation time: 30 minutes

150 g/5 oz wheatgerm
150 g/5 oz porridge oats
60 g/2 oz almonds or hazelnuts, chopped
60 g/2 oz demerera sugar
45 g/1½ oz sesame seeds
45 g/1½ oz sunflower seeds
30 g/1 oz desiccated coconut
90 ml/3 fl oz groundnut oil
½ teaspoon vanilla extract

This is based on a wonderful recipe from Cherida Cannon, who runs Bonhams Farm bed and breakfast in Alton, Hampshire.

Preheat the oven to 180°C/350°F/gas mark 4. Place all of the ingredients along with 4 tablespoons of water into a large mixing bowl. Stir well to combine and transfer to a very large shallow baking tray. Spread the mixture evenly so that it is in a thin layer. If you don't have a tray big enough you can use 2 smaller ones and swap them over in the oven halfway through the cooking time.

Place in the oven for 25 minutes or until the granola is golden brown. Stir every now and then during the cooking time to ensure it browns evenly. Take out of the oven and set aside to cool. Transfer to a large airtight jar for storage. Serve with icy cold milk or creamy yoghurt.

Raw muesli

Serves 6
Preparation time: 5 minutes

90 g/3 oz bran sticks
60 g/2 oz wheat germ
120 g/4 oz jumbo oats
90 g/3 oz rye flakes
45 g/1½ oz pecan nuts
45 g/1½ oz hazelnuts
60 g/2 oz dried pitted dates, chopped
60 g/2 oz dried apple, chopped

This fibre-filled muesli will fill you up for hours. It can be made in no time, and all of the ingredients can be found in health food shops.

For a more substantial breakfast try topping a bowlful with slices of banana, a dollop of yoghurt and a spoonful of honey.

Place all of the ingredients in a large mixing bowl and stir them well to combine.

Brown sugar and vanilla porridge with caramelised bananas

Serves 2
Preparation time: 15 minutes

75 g/2½ oz porridge oats
240 ml/8 fl oz milk
pinch sea salt
¼ teaspoon vanilla extract
2 tablespoons plus 1 teaspoon soft brown sugar,
    preferably a darker variety
15 g/½ oz butter
1 large banana, peeled and cut into thick diagonal slices

Transform plain old porridge into something irresistible with sticky brown-sugar-coated bananas and a dash of vanilla extract – yum!

Place the oats, milk and salt in a pan and add 240 ml/8 fl oz water. Stir well, set over a medium heat and bring to the boil. Turn down the heat, stir and simmer for 3 minutes, stirring often. Add the vanilla and 2 tablespoons of the sugar and stir through. Take off the heat and cover the pan while you cook the banana slices.

Heat the butter in a non-stick frying pan placed over a medium heat until it begins to bubble. Add the banana slices and cook for a minute on each side or until they are nicely browned at the edges. Gently remove the banana slices from the pan onto a plate, leaving the butter in the bottom of the pan. Sprinkle the remaining sugar in the pan, stirring until the sugar dissolves. Return the banana slices to the pan and gently shake the pan around to coat the slices in the caramelised sugar. Tip the banana slices and any pan juices back onto the plate as they will carry on cooking if you leave them in the hot pan.

Divide the porridge into 2 warmed bowls, top with the caramelised banana slices and any remaining pan juices and serve immediately.

Coconut and palm sugar rice pudding

Serves 4
Preparation time: 45 minutes

400 ml/14 fl oz coconut milk
200 ml/7 fl oz milk
4 tablespoons liquid palm sugar, plus extra to serve
90 g/3 oz pudding rice
large pinch sea salt
1 heaped tablespoon shredded coconut, toasted

This Thai inspired, rich and creamy rice pudding is a great winter warmer. Try serving it in authentic Oriental rice cups.

Palm sugar is a thick, often dark sugar made from palm sap. Available in Oriental grocery stores, it is usually sold in large solid lumps. You can either hammer away at it or place the whole lot in a pan with a little water so it melts into a pourable syrup.

Place the coconut milk, milk, palm sugar, rice and salt in a small heavy-based saucepan set over a high heat. Stir well and bring to the boil, then turn the heat down to the lowest setting. Cook for 40 minutes, stirring often, until the rice is cooked and the liquid becomes thick and creamy.

Divide the rice among 4 small bowls and pour a little palm sugar over the top. Sprinkle with the toasted coconut and serve immediately.

Sweet couscous with pomegranate seeds, dried berries and pine nuts

Serves 4
Preparation time: 25 minutes

180 g/6 oz couscous
¼ teaspoon ground cinnamon, plus extra to serve
1 tablespoon light olive oil
2 tablespoons icing sugar, plus extra to serve
180 ml/6 fl oz boiling water
15 g/½ oz pumpkin seeds
60 g/2 oz pomegranate seeds
30 g/1 oz dried berries
30 g/1 oz pine nuts, toasted
4 heaped tablespoons buttermilk or yoghurt, to serve

Place the couscous, cinnamon, olive oil and icing sugar into a mixing bowl and stir well to combine. Cover with the boiling water, stir to make sure the couscous is under the water then cover and leave for 10 minutes.

Use a fork to break up any lumps of couscous then tip onto a tray to cool for 5 minutes, stirring through with a fork a few more times whilst it cools. Add most of the pumpkin seeds, pomegranate seeds, dried berries and pine nuts, reserving a few of each to serve on top. Stir well to combine then transfer to 4 bowls and dust with a little cinnamon and icing sugar. Sprinkle with the reserved toppings, top with the buttermilk or yoghurt and serve.

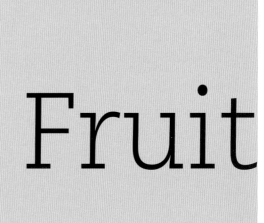

Fruit

Stone fruit salad with stem ginger and orange fromage frais

Serves 6
Preparation time: 10 minutes

200 g/7 oz cherries
2 nectarines
2 plums
2 peaches
2 large apricots
juice of ½ orange
300 g/10½ oz fromage frais
2 tablespoons stem ginger syrup
2 teaspoons finely chopped stem ginger
finely grated zest of 1 orange

This fruit salad calls for perfectly ripe, sweet and juicy stone fruits.

Pit the cherries – this takes no time with an olive stoner – and place in a mixing bowl. Halve the remaining fruits, take out the stones and cut each half in 4 wedges. Place the fruit wedges in the bowl with the cherries and toss carefully with the orange juice.

Place the fromage frais, stem ginger syrup and chopped ginger, and the orange zest in a small bowl and stir well.

Divide the fruit salad among 6 small bowls and top with a dollop of the fromage frais.

Tropical fruit platter with chilli, lime and coconut

Serves 6
Preparation time: 15 minutes

2 large or 8 tiny bananas, peeled and sliced if large, halved if small
1 small papaya, peeled, deseeded and sliced
1 small mango, peeled, deseeded and sliced
1 small pineapple, peeled and sliced
1 starfruit, sliced
2 tablespoons lime juice
1½ teaspoons soft brown sugar (optional)
1 teaspoon finely sliced red chilli
1 lime leaf, very finely sliced
2 tablespoons coconut shavings, toasted
1 whole lime, cut in 6 wedges

The success of this fruit platter relies on super sweet, fragrantly ripe and lightly chilled fruit. Nothing less than supermodel specimens will do. For a tropical theme, try arranging the fruit on a length of fresh banana leaf; these are available from Oriental grocers.

Randomly arrange the fruit slices on a large platter and pour the lime juice on top. Sprinkle over the sugar, if using, and top with the chilli, lime leaf and coconut shavings. Arrange the lime wedges on the platter and serve.

Baked ricotta cheese with grilled figs and honey

Serves 6
Preparation time: 1 hour 10 minutes

500 g/1 lb 2 oz ricotta cheese, drained of excess liquid
2 large free-range eggs, lightly beaten
3 tablespoons honey, plus extra for serving
finely grated zest of 1 lemon
6 large ripe, juicy figs

Preheat the oven to 180°C/350°F/gas mark 4. Place the ricotta in a mixing bowl with the eggs, honey and lemon zest and beat with a wooden spoon until smooth.

Lightly oil a loaf tin and pour in the mixture. Place the filled loaf tin in a roasting tin. Pour enough warm water in the roasting tin to come about halfway up the sides of the loaf tin. Gently transfer to the oven and cook for 45 minutes. Carefully remove the loaf tin and set aside to cool for 15 minutes. Turn the baked ricotta out of the tin onto on a serving plate with the cooked side up. The loaf can be eaten at this stage, or refrigerated and eaten chilled.

Preheat a large griddle pan over a high heat. Cut the figs in half and place them flesh side down on the griddle pan for 1–2 minutes or until coloured. Turn them over and repeat on the other side.

Serve slices of baked ricotta with the grilled figs and a good drizzling of honey.

Saffron-spiced dried fruit salad

Serves 4
Preparation time: 5 minutes, plus 1 hour infusing time

90 g/3 oz dried figs, stalks removed
90 g/3 oz dried apricots, pitted
30 g/1 oz dried apple rings
90 g/3 oz dried dates, pitted
pinch saffron threads
1 cinnamon stick, broken in half
3 cardamom pods, lightly bruised
2 cloves
1 tablespoon honey
thick yoghurt, to serve

This healthy mix of plump dried fruit is transformed by the exotic flavours and aroma of saffron, cloves, cinnamon and cardamom. Try serving it with a handful of chopped walnuts, almonds or pistachios.

Place the figs, apricots, apple rings and dates in a heatproof mixing bowl. Put the saffron, cinnamon, cardamom, cloves and honey in a small pan with 250 ml/9 fl oz water. Set over a low heat until it reaches a gentle simmer. Take off the heat and pour the liquid over the dried fruit. Stir well then cover the bowl and leave for 1 hour for the flavours to infuse, and to soften the fruit.

Remove the cinnamon sticks, cardamom and cloves. Serve the fruits and their liquid chilled or at room temperature, with a dollop of yoghurt.

Rhubarb and strawberry compote

Serves 4–6
Preparation time: 20 minutes, plus cooling time

370 g/13 oz rhubarb, washed, trimmed and
   cut into 2.5 cm/1 inch lengths
4 tablespoons orange juice,
3 strips orange zest
3–4 slices fresh ginger, peeled
4 tablespoons caster sugar
200 g/7 oz strawberries, washed, hulled and halved

Try serving this sweet scented compote with thick
yoghurt and a handful of toasted muesli.

Place the rhubarb, orange juice and zest, ginger and caster
sugar in a saucepan over a high heat. Stir well, allow the
mixture to bubble then cover the pan. Turn down the heat to
low and simmer for 5 minutes. Add the strawberries to the
pan, gently stir, cover and cook for a further 3 minutes or
until the fruit softens but retains its shape.
   Transfer to a large heatproof bowl and set aside to cool.
   Once cooled, discard the orange zest and ginger slices.
Serve the compote chilled or at room temperature.

Wild strawberry and vanilla yoghurt

Serves 4
Preparation time: 10 minutes

200 g/7 oz wild strawberries
500 g/1 lb 2 oz Greek yoghurt
seeds of 1 vanilla pod
2 heaped tablespoons icing sugar, sifted

Known in their native France as fraises des bois, these
intoxicatingly fragrant wild strawberries are a real
treat. They have a ridiculously short shelf-life which
dictates their high price. You can use super sweet
strawberries for a perfectly acceptable variation of
this recipe, although the intensity of the fraises des
bois cannot be replicated.

Place most of the berries in a food processor, reserving a few
for garnish. Whizz until you get a thick purée and set aside
until needed.
   Place the yoghurt in a large mixing bowl. Beat in the
vanilla seeds and icing sugar until well combined. Pour in the
strawberry purée and gently fold it into the yoghurt to get a
slightly rippled effect. Spoon into 4 small bowls and top with
the reserved berries.

Vanilla poached white nectarines

Serves 6
Preparation time: 20 minutes

200 g/7 oz caster sugar
1 vanilla pod, split lengthwise
6 large white nectarines
Greek yoghurt, to serve

These glossy, rose-hued nectarines are a real treat. You can use regular nectarines if you can't track down the white ones. Alternatively, white or yellow peaches will do the trick.

Place the caster sugar, vanilla pod and 900 ml/1½ pints cold water in a saucepan large enough to accommodate the nectarines snugly in a single layer. Set the pan over a low heat and stir until the sugar dissolves. When the liquid starts to form tiny bubbles, turn up the heat to medium and add the nectarines. Cover the pan, turn the heat down to low and simmer for 7 minutes, gently turning the nectarines over halfway through the cooking time. Remove the nectarines with a slotted spoon and set aside while you reduce the cooking liquid.

Lift the vanilla pod from the cooking liquid with a slotted spoon and scrape the seeds into the pan. Add the pod, turn the heat up to high and bring to the boil. Cook for 5 minutes or until the liquid becomes a light syrup. Take the pan off the heat and allow the syrup to cool slightly.

Peel the nectarines, discard the skin and place them in a large serving bowl. Pour the syrup over the nectarines and allow it to cool to room temperature. Serve the poached nectarines and their syrup cold or at room temperature with a dollop of Greek yoghurt.

Watermelon with feta cheese and mint

Serves 4
Preparation time: 5 minutes

800 g/1 lb 12 oz watermelon flesh, chilled
200 g/7 oz feta cheese
10 large mint leaves, roughly chopped

to serve
olive oil
lime juice
freshly ground black pepper

Sounds unusual, but the combination of salty feta, sweet watermelon and zingy mint is a deliciously refreshing one.

Cut the watermelon in large cubes, removing as many seeds as you can. Place in a large serving bowl.

Crumble the feta cheese over the watermelon and top with the chopped mint. Sprinkle over some olive oil and lime juice and top with a few grindings of black pepper. Toss lightly and serve.

Baked apples with sultanas, honey and almonds

Serves 4
Preparation time: 50 minutes

4 small to medium apples
15 g/½ oz melted butter,
   plus extra for brushing
1 heaped tablespoon honey
pinch ground nutmeg
pinch ground ginger
pinch ground cinnamon
60 g/2 oz sultanas
15 g/½ oz blanched almonds,
   toasted and roughly chopped
thick yoghurt, to serve

A perfect breakfast for a chilly winter morning, the addition of nutmeg, ginger and cinnamon give this dish a gentle spicy twist. Serve the apples with spoonfuls of thick yoghurt and wake up slowly while you eat. For best results, use smallish cooking apples, such as Empire or Braeburn.

Preheat the oven to 200°C/400°F/gas mark 6. Use an apple corer to remove the core and pips of the apples. You will be left with a long hollow through the middle of each apple in which to hold the stuffing. Score the circumference of each apple with a small sharp knife. This will prevent them from splitting during cooking.

Place the remaining ingredients in a small bowl and stir to combine. Stuff the mixture in the apples, pressing down with your fingers to compact the stuffing firmly. Lightly brush the apples and a small baking dish with melted butter. Place the stuffed apples in the dish and bake in the oven for 30 minutes. Take out of the oven, baste the apples with the juices in the bottom of the baking dish and return to the oven for a further 10 minutes or until the apples are cooked through. Serve hot or warm with a spoon of thick yoghurt.

Home
Bakes

Fig and hazelnut focaccia

Makes one 30 cm/12 inch round focaccia
Preparation time: 1 hour, plus 1 hour proving time

750 g/1 lb 11 oz strong white flour, plus extra for dusting
7 g/¼ oz sachet dried yeast
2 teaspoons sea salt
2 tablespoons vegetable oil, plus a little extra for greasing
2 tablespoons honey
250 g/9 oz semi-dried figs, stems discarded and halved
   or quartered
120 g/4 oz hazelnuts, lightly toasted

This fruity nutty focaccia is best cut into wedges or slices and smeared with butter and honey. It can be served fresh, toasted or char-grilled. It will keep for a while if well covered, and any leftovers can be frozen.

It is important to use semi-dried figs, as their sweet squidgy flesh breaks up during kneading, dispersing the tiny fig seeds through the focaccia.

Place the flour, yeast and salt into a large mixing bowl, keeping the yeast and salt away from each other so they don't react too soon. Mix the oil and honey with 400 ml/14 fl oz tepid water and add to the dry mixture. Mix the dough with your hands until the ingredients are incorporated then transfer to a lightly floured board and knead for 8 minutes or until the dough is smooth and stretchy. For a quicker result you can place the dry mixture into a mixer or food processor with the dough hook attached then slowly pour in the liquid and process until the dough is smooth and elastic.

Lightly brush the inside of a large mixing bowl with oil. Roll the dough into a ball and place in the oiled bowl, covering with a cloth. Transfer to a warm place and allow the dough to rise until it doubles in size. This should take about an hour, but can vary depending on the room temperature.

Preheat the oven to 220°C/430°F/gas mark 7. Oil a baking sheet. Place the risen dough on a floured board. Roughly roll or stretch the dough to create a large surface area, then scatter over the figs and nuts. Knead the dough well to incorporate the figs and nuts and to 'knock out' the air bubbles that made the dough rise. This will take a few minutes and the dough will be a little sticky as the figs will have broken up in the kneading. Once incorporated, re-flour the board and roll or stretch the dough into a rough 30 cm/12 inch circle. Transfer the dough circle to the oiled baking sheet and press into a neat circle with your hands. Use your fingertips to make lots of large deep indents all over the dough, then transfer to the oven and cook for 25 minutes, loosely covering the focaccia with foil for the last 10 minutes. When it is cooked, the base of the focaccia should sound hollow when tapped.

Allow the focaccia to cool then cut into wedges and serve, toasted or untoasted.

Polenta, raspberry and yoghurt cakes

Makes 10
Preparation time: 45 minutes

90 g/3 oz golden caster sugar
150 g/5 oz polenta
90 g/3 oz soft butter
2 large free-range eggs
90 g/3 oz yoghurt
90 g/3 oz ground almonds
zest of 1 lemon, finely grated
1 heaped teaspoon baking powder
150 g/5 oz raspberries

icing
120 g/4 oz icing sugar
30 g/1 oz raspberries
1 teaspoon yoghurt
lemon juice for thinning the icing

Not just a pretty face. The polenta in these sweet little cakes gives them a lovely texture with its characteristic grittiness.

Preheat the oven to 180°C/350°F/gas mark 4. Lightly oil a 10-cup muffin tin or 10 small cake moulds.

Place the sugar, polenta and butter in a large mixing bowl and beat until combined. Add the eggs, yoghurt, almonds, lemon zest and baking powder and beat to incorporate. Gently fold in the berries and divide the mixture among the muffin cups or cake moulds. The cakes will rise a little so allow a small gap when filling. Firmly tap the filled muffin tin or moulds to remove any air bubbles.

Bake in the oven for 20 minutes then remove and leave the cakes to cool for a few minutes. Gently unmould the warm cakes and place on a cooling rack. Allow to cool to room temperature before icing them.

To make the icing, sift the icing sugar into a mixing bowl. Place the berries in a small bowl and mash with a fork. Transfer the mashed berries to a tea strainer and strain the liquid over the icing sugar. There will not be a lot, but you need only enough to colour the icing. Add the yoghurt and stir the mixture until you have a thick pink paste. Add enough lemon juice to make a slightly runny but not too liquid icing. You may need only a few drops. If you add too much you can add some more sifted icing sugar to thicken it. Spoon the icing over the cakes and allow it to set.

Chocolate orange soured cream muffins

Makes 10 muffins
Preparation time: 30 minutes

90 g/3 oz soft butter
90 g/3 oz golden caster sugar
2 large free-range eggs
150 ml/5 fl oz soured cream
150 g/5 oz plain flour
1 teaspoon baking powder
pinch salt
90 g/3 oz dark chocolate with 70% solids, roughly chopped
zest of 1 orange, grated

Preheat the oven to 180°C/350°F/gas mark 4. Line a 10-cup muffin tin with paper muffin cases.

Place all the ingredients into a large mixing bowl and beat with an electric whisk until incorporated. Spoon the mixture into the muffin cases. The mixture will not completely fill the cases, to allow it to rise during cooking.

Cook in the oven for 20 minutes or until the muffins are well risen and lightly browned. Gently remove the muffins in their cases from the tin and put on a cooling rack. Serve slightly warm or at room temperature.

Banana and coconut teacake with maple, vanilla and allspice butter

Makes 1 loaf, about 8–10 slices
Preparation time: 1 hour 15 minutes

150 g/5 oz fresh coconut flesh, grated
3 very ripe bananas (about 240 g/8 oz peeled weight)
120 g/4 oz soft butter
120 g/4 oz golden caster sugar
3 large free-range eggs
240 g/8 oz plain flour
1½ teaspoons baking powder
1 teaspoon ground cinnamon
pinch sea salt

maple, vanilla and allspice butter
1 teaspoon vanilla extract
120 g/4 oz soft butter
1 tablespoon maple syrup
large pinch ground allspice, or a little more if you
    like it spicy

This super-moist teacake will last for a few days if well wrapped.

Preheat the oven to 180°C/360°F/gas mark 4. Grease and line a loaf tin and set aside.

Place the coconut and banana into a food processor and blitz to a purée. Put the butter and sugar into a large mixing bowl and beat with an electric whisk until pale. Add the eggs, flour, baking powder, cinnamon and salt along with the puréed coconut and banana and beat until incorporated. Place the batter into the prepared loaf tin and tap it down firmly to remove any air bubbles. Bake in the oven for 1 hour, covering the teacake for the last 15 minutes to stop it colouring too much. Allow to cool slightly in the tin then transfer to a cooling rack. Eat warm or at room temperature.

Meanwhile, make the butter. Place all the ingredients into a bowl and beat or whisk until smooth.

Slice the cake thickly and spread with the butter.

Mocha almond biscotti

Makes 24
Preparation time: 1 hour 30 minutes

1 large free-range egg
90 g/3 oz plain flour, plus extra for shaping the dough
120 g/4 oz golden caster sugar, plus a teaspoon for
    sprinkling over the biscotti
1 teaspoon instant coffee dissolved in 1 tablespoon hot water
5 tablespoons best quality cocoa
½ teaspoon baking powder
½ teaspoon vanilla extract
large pinch salt
60 g/2 oz blanched almonds
milk, for glazing the biscotti

These twice-baked crunchy biscuits are perfect for
dunking into coffee, hot chocolate or even a glass of
icy cold milk.

Preheat the oven to 180°C/360°F/gas mark 4 and cover a
baking sheet with non-stick baking paper. Place all the
ingredients except the almonds and milk into a mixing bowl
and mix with a wooden spoon until combined. At first it will
appear quite dry but will soon become a thick sticky dough.
Mix in the almonds until they are evenly distributed – this
will take a minute or so as the dough is very dense.

Turn out onto a well-floured board and sprinkle liberally
with flour. Working quickly with floured hands, roll the
dough into a log roughly 6 x 22 cm/2½ x 8½ inch. Carefully
transfer the log to the lined baking sheet. Brush it with a
little milk and sprinkle with a teaspoon of sugar. Place in
the oven for 30 minutes then remove. Turn the oven down
to 140°C/280°F/gas mark 1½. Leave the log to cool for
15 minutes.

Transfer the log to a cutting board and gently cut into
24 slices with a sharp bread knife. If the knife is not sharp
enough it will crush rather than slice the log. Lay the biscotti
slices sideways onto the baking sheet and place in the oven
for 30 minutes or until completely dried out. Allow the
biscotti to cool completely then store in an airtight container.

Pumpkin, feta and rosemary buttermilk scones

Makes 12
Preparation time: 1 hour

250 g/9 oz pumpkin or butternut squash, peeled
    and cut into 1.5cm/½ inch cubes
1 tablespoon olive oil
sea salt and freshly ground black pepper
250 g/9 oz self-raising flour, plus extra for dusting
1 teaspoon bicarbonate of soda
60 g/2 oz cold butter, cubed
180 ml/6 fl oz buttermilk
1 heaped tablespoon rosemary leaves, chopped
120 g/4 oz feta cheese, cut into 1.5 cm/½ inch cubes

These tasty savoury scones are best eaten warm
with lashings of butter, or they can be served with
proscuitto slices for a weekend brunch.

Preheat the oven to 200°C/400°F/gas mark 6. Place the
pumpkin or squash and olive oil into a bowl and season well.
Toss to coat in the oil and tip out into a small roasting tin.
Cook in the oven for 30 minutes or until tender and lightly
coloured. Set aside to cool.

Increase the oven temperature to 225°C/240°F/gas
mark 7½. Put the flour, bicarbonate of soda, butter,
½ teaspoon salt and few grindings of pepper into a food
processor and whizz to the consistency of breadcrumbs.
Tip into a mixing bowl and fold in the buttermilk, rosemary
and cheese to make a sticky dough. Liberally flour a work
surface or board and place the dough in the middle. Flour
the top of the dough well and gently roll out to a thickness
of 2.5cm/1 inch. Using a 6 cm/2½ inch fluted scone cutter,
cut out 12 scones, gently re-rolling the off-cuts as you go.
Place the scones on a lightly oiled baking sheet and cook for
12 minutes. Remove from the oven and eat hot, warm or at
room temperature.

Bacon, shallot and jalapeño pepper muffins

Makes 8
Preparation time: 50 minutes

1 tablespoon olive oil
75 g/2½ oz smoked bacon, chopped
2 large shallots, peeled and finely chopped
7 tablespoons milk
2 large free-range eggs
150 g/5 oz plain flour
1 teaspoon baking powder
¼ teaspoon sea salt
¼ teaspoon sugar
¾ teaspoon smoked paprika
60 g/2 oz soft butter
1 heaped tablespoon pickled jalapeño peppers, chopped

These flavoursome muffins need little in the way
of accompaniments – a generous smear of butter or
cream cheese. Pickled japaleño peppers are available
from most supermarkets. If you substitute chopped
fresh chillies, go easy on the quantity.

Preheat the oven to 180°C/350°F/gas mark 4 and lightly oil
or butter 8 holes of a muffin pan. Place the olive oil in a
frying pan set over a medium heat and add the bacon. Cook
for 4–5 minutes or until the bacon is slightly crispy, then
remove with a slotted spoon (leaving the fat in the pan) and
set aside. Turn the heat down and cook the shallots for
5 minutes or until they soften, then add them to the bacon.

Place the milk and eggs in a small bowl and whisk with
a fork. Sift the flour and other dry ingredients into a large
mixing bowl. Add the butter and use an electric whisk to
combine the mixture until it resembles rough breadcrumbs.
Whisk in the eggy mixture until you have a smooth batter.
Fold in the bacon, shallots and jalapeño peppers with a large
spoon. Divide the batter between the oiled muffin holes.
Bake in the oven for 25 minutes or until a skewer inserted in
a muffin comes out clean. Remove from the oven and gently
turn the muffins out onto a cooking rack. Eat hot or warm.

Bacon and quails egg flan with crème fraîche and chives

Serves 4
Preparation time: 25 minutes

plain flour for dusting
275 g/10 oz puff pastry
9–12 quails eggs
75g /2½ oz crème fraîche
small handful of long chives
150 g/5 oz thinly sliced smoked streaky bacon,
   rind removed
freshly ground black pepper

This is heaven on a pastry base. The smoked bacon
and gooey eggs are perfectly suited to the slight
tartness of the crème fraiche and the oniony chives.

Preheat the oven to 220°C/425°F/gas mark 7. Lightly flour
a work surface and roll the pastry out into a rectangle a little
larger than an A4 piece of paper. Then cut out a piece the
size of an A4 piece of paper. The reason for this is that the
pastry edges will rise more evenly if cut to size rather than
rolled. Transfer the pastry to a lightly oiled baking sheet then
use a sharp knife to score a 1 cm/½ inch border inside the
edge of the pastry. Prick the pastry inside the border with a
fork – this will be the area that is covered with the toppings.

Whisk one egg lightly and use it to brush the pastry
border. Smear the crème fraîche inside the pastry border,
covering the whole rectangle evenly. Scatter half of the chive
lengths on top and arrange the bacon rashers side by side to
cover the crème fraîche.

Bake for 12 minutes then remove from the oven and place
the baking sheet on a flat surface. Randomly break the eggs
on top of the bacon then season with black pepper. Return
the flan to the oven for 3 minutes or until the egg whites set.
Gently transfer to a board or platter and scatter with the
remaining chives. Slice into large pieces and eat hot or warm.

Hot
Sweet
Stuff

Crumpets with honeycomb

Makes 14–16 x 9 cm/3½ inch crumpets
Preparation time: 1 hour 15 minutes, plus 2 hours
resting time

325 g/11 oz plain flour
7 g/¼ oz sachet dry yeast
1 teaspoon caster sugar
450 ml/16 fl oz skimmed milk, warmed until it is 'hand hot'
½ teaspoon bicarbonate of soda
1 teaspoon sea salt
vegetable oil, for brushing the pan
butter and honeycomb, to serve

Place the flour, yeast and sugar into a large mixing bowl. Add 350 ml/12 fl oz of the warmed milk and mix with an electric beaters until smooth. Cover the bowl and set aside until the batter doubles in size. This should take about an hour.

Pour the remaining milk into a bowl and whisk in the bicarbonate of soda and salt. Pour this into the batter and whisk again until incorporated. The batter will be stringy and gloopy – but this is how it should be. Set aside and allow the batter to rest for 30 minutes, by which time it will be bubbly. Add 200 ml/7 fl oz water to the batter and whisk until incorporated, then set aside for a further 30 minutes or until it is bubbly again. Once the batter is at this stage, it can sit around for an hour or two.

Place a large heavy-based frying pan over a low heat. It is best to do this over the largest stove ring so that the heat is consistent over the entire surface of the pan. Lightly brush the pan and 4 crumpet rings or 9 cm/3½ inch round cutters with vegetable oil. Place the 4 rings or cutters in the pan and add 3½–4 tablespoons of batter to each one. Cook for 8–10 minutes or until the surface is bubbling and full of holes, and the bases are browned. The bases will be quite dark (but not burnt) and hard but will soften once they cool. Remove the rings and turn the crumpets over, cooking the other side for a further few minutes or until golden brown. Transfer the crumpets to a wire rack and repeat with the rest of the batter.

Eat hot or warm, or allow the crumpets to cool and toast them before eating. Top with butter and honeycomb and serve.

Raspberry yoghurt pikelets with vanilla mascarpone

Serves 4
Preparation time: 40 minutes

maple vanilla mascarpone
150 g/5 oz mascarpone cheese, at room temperature
¼ teaspoon vanilla extract
2 tablespoons icing sugar, sifted

pikelets
4 tablespoons yoghurt
4 tablespoons milk
finely grated zest of 1 lemon
2 large free-range eggs, separated
3 tablespoons caster sugar
30 g/1 oz melted butter
150 g/5 oz plain flour
1 teaspoon baking powder
pinch fine sea salt
75 g/2½ oz raspberries, plus extra to serve
butter for cooking

Put the mascarpone, vanilla and icing sugar in a bowl and beat until smooth. Cover and refrigerate.

For the pikelets, put the yoghurt, milk, lemon zest, egg yolks, sugar and melted butter in a large mixing bowl and whisk lightly. Sift in the flour, baking powder and salt and whisk until smooth. Set aside to rest for 10 minutes.

Place a large non-stick frying pan over a medium heat. Put the egg whites in a mixing bowl and beat with an electric whisk until stiff. Gently fold the raspberries into the batter followed by the stiffened egg whites.

Place a small knob of butter in the pan and swirl it around to lightly coat the base. Add 2 tablespoons of the batter to make an 8–9 cm/3–3½ inch pancake. Repeat 3 times so you have 4 small pikelets. Cook for 1–2 minutes or until small bubbles form on the top. Turn the pikelets over and cook for a further 1–2 minutes. Remove and keep warm. Wipe out the pan and repeat the process to make 12 pikelets in total. Serve immediately with the mascarpone and a few raspberries.

Churros con chocolate

Serves 4
Preparation time: 40 minutes plus 15 minutes
for the hot chocolate

90 g/3 oz caster sugar
1 teaspoon ground cinnamon
200 g/7 oz strong plain flour
¼ teaspoon salt
1 large free-range egg
vegetable oil for deep-frying

Mix the caster sugar and cinnamon together and place on
a large serving plate.

Pour 400 ml/14 fl oz water into a pan set over a high heat
and bring to a rolling boil. Add the flour and salt, take off
the heat and beat vigorously with a wooden spoon for about
1 minute until the flour is absorbed. Do not expect a smooth
mixture – it will be pasty, a little like gloopy mashed potato.

Set aside to cool for 15 minutes, then beat in the egg.
At first it will appear as if the egg will not incorporate into
the mixture but it just takes a little perseverance.

Heat the oil in a large pan or deep-fryer. Place the dough
mixture into a large strong piping bag with a star tip nozzle
attached. Carefully squeeze out the dough (it will be quite
firm) over the hot oil and cut into 15–20 cm/6–8 inch
lengths with scissors. Allow the dough strips to fall into
the oil but avoid doing this from too much of a height,
to prevent splashing. Cook about 4 churros at a time for
3–4 minutes, turning once until they are golden brown.
Drain on kitchen paper. Repeat with the remaining mixture.
You should get about 12 churros in total, depending on their
length and the width of the nozzle. Roll the churros in the
cinnamon sugar and serve with hot chocolate (see opposite).

Hot chocolate

Serves 4
Preparation time: 15 minutes

500 ml/18 fl oz milk
120 g/4 oz dark chocolate, chopped or grated
1 teaspoon cornflour
1 tablespoon caster sugar, or to taste

This thickened hot chocolate does not require a high-
grade, super-duper bitter gourmet chocolate. Regular
sweet dark chocolate works just fine.

Warm the milk in a pan set over a medium heat. Add the
chocolate and stir until melted. Measure the cornflour into
a small bowl and add 2 tablespoons of the hot chocolate.
Whisk well to incorporate the cornflour and pour the
mixture back into the pan of hot chocolate. Cook for 4–5
minutes, stirring often, until it is the thickness of double
cream. Stir in sugar to taste and pour the hot chocolate into
4 small heatproof cups to serve.

Brioche French toast with cherry, vanilla and cinnamon compote

Serves 4
Preparation time: 30 minutes

cherry and cinnamon compote
3 tablespoons vanilla sugar
2 teaspoons lemon juice
1 cinnamon stick, broken in half
250 g/9 oz cherries, pitted

french toast
1 large free-range egg, plus 1 yolk
150 ml/5 fl oz milk
2 tablespoons caster sugar
4 thick slices brioche
30 g/1 oz butter

If you don't have vanilla sugar use caster sugar and add a few drops of pure vanilla extract to the recipe.

For the compote, place the vanilla sugar, lemon juice and cinnamon stick in a small pan with 6 tablespoons of water. Set over a medium heat, stir and bring to a simmer. Add the cherries, cover the pan and lower the heat. Cook for 5 minutes or until the cherries soften but retain their shape. Remove the cherries with a slotted spoon and place them in a bowl. Turn up the heat and bring the liquid to the boil. Cook for a few minutes until it is slightly syrupy. Pour over the cherries and set aside while you prepare the French toast.

  Place the egg, extra yolk, milk and sugar in a wide shallow bowl and whisk to combine. Set a large non-stick frying pan over a medium heat. Place the brioche slices in the eggy mixture and turn over to coat both sides. Leave to soak while you add about half of the butter to the hot pan. Place the soaked brioche slices in the pan. Cook for 2 minutes or until nicely browned. Turn the brioche slices over, adding some or all of the remaining butter to the pan if necessary. Cook for a further 2 minutes or until golden brown. Place on 4 plates and top with the cherries and their syrup.

Vanilla waffles with white chocolate sauce and fresh strawberries

Serves 4–6, depending on the waffle machine capacity
Preparation time: 35–40 minutes

white chocolate sauce
150 ml/5 fl oz whipping cream
75 g/2½ oz best quality white chocolate, finely chopped

waffles
3 large free-range eggs, separated
360 ml/13 fl oz milk
90 g/3 oz butter, melted
1 teaspoon vanilla extract
270 g/9½ oz plain flour
large pinch fine sea salt
2 tablespoons caster sugar
2 teaspoons baking powder
350 g/12 oz strawberries, hulled and halved

For the white chocolate sauce, place the cream and chocolate in a small heatproof bowl and set over a small pan of barely simmering water. Leave for 3–4 minutes to allow the chocolate to melt, then stir until the sauce is smooth. Turn off the heat, keeping the bowl of sauce over the pan to stay warm while you prepare the waffles.

  For the waffles, preheat a waffle maker. Place the egg yolks in a large mixing bowl with the milk, butter and vanilla and whisk to combine. Sift the flour, salt, sugar and baking powder together and beat this into the milky mixture until you have a thick, smooth batter. Put the egg whites in a mixing bowl and beat with an electric whisk until stiff. Gently fold into the batter.

  Place some of the batter in the waffle maker and cook according to the manufacturer's instructions. Remove the cooked waffle and keep warm while you prepare the rest. A domestic waffle maker should make 4–6 waffles.

  Serve the warm waffles with the white chocolate sauce and a handful of strawberries.

Buttermilk pancakes with pecan and maple butter

Serves 4
Preparation time: 40 minutes

pecan maple butter
60 g/2 oz salted butter, softened
15 g/½ oz toasted pecan nuts, finely chopped
3 tablespoons maple syrup, plus extra for serving

pancakes
8 tablespoons buttermilk
8 tablespoons milk
2 large free-range eggs, separated
2 tablespoons caster sugar
30 g/1 oz butter, melted
180 g/6 oz plain flour
2 teaspoons baking powder
large pinch fine sea salt
butter for cooking

For the pecan maple butter, put the butter, pecans and maple syrup in a bowl and beat until well combined. Set aside to chill while you prepare the pancakes.

Put the buttermilk, milk, egg yolks, sugar and melted butter in a mixing bowl and whisk lightly. Sift the flour, baking powder and salt together and whisk into the liquid to make a thick, smooth batter. Set aside to rest for 10 minutes.

Place a large non-stick frying pan over a medium heat. Put the egg whites in a mixing bowl and beat with an electric whisk until stiff. Gently fold into the batter.

Place a small knob of butter in the pan and swirl it around to lightly coat the base. Add 3 tablespoons of the batter to make an 11 cm/4½ inch pancake. Repeat twice – you should be able to cook 3 at a time in a large pan.

Cook for 2–3 minutes or until small bubbles form in the pancake. Turn the pancakes over and cook the other side for a further minute or two. Wipe out the pan after each batch and keep the pancakes warm while you use up the remaining mixture. You should have 8 in total. Serve the hot pancakes with maple syrup and a dollop of pecan maple butter.

Crêpes with caramelised pears

Serves 4
Preparation time: 45 minutes, plus 30 minutes resting time

crêpes
6 tablespoons soured cream
75 g/2½ oz plain flour
2 large free-range eggs
1 tablespoon caster sugar
pinch fine sea salt
2 tablespoons melted butter
extra butter for cooking the crêpes
soured cream, crème fraiche or lightly whipped cream,
    to serve

caramelised pears
4 small ripe pears
15 g/½ oz butter
3 tablespoons soft brown sugar
pinch ground cardamom

For the crêpes, place the soured cream, flour, eggs, sugar, salt and melted butter in a blender with 6 tablespoons of water. Whizz until smooth then pour into a jug, cover and leave to rest for 30 minutes.

Place a non-stick crêpe or frying pan over a medium heat and add a knob of butter. Pour about 4 tablespoons of the batter into the pan and swirl the pan to distribute the batter. Cook for a minute or until lightly browned, then gently turn over using a spatula. Cook for a further minute, then set aside on a plate. Make 8 crêpes, stacking them as they are cooked. Keep them warm while you prepare the pears.

Peel the pears then quarter and core them. Place the butter in a large non-stick frying pan over a medium high heat. Cook the pears for 3 minutes or until lightly coloured. Turn them over and cook for a few minutes on the other side. Add the sugar and cardamom and toss the pears until they are well coated. Cook for 1– 2 minutes or until the pears are tender. Serve the pears and their juices with the crêpes, with a dollop of soured cream, crème fraiche or whipped cream.

Sandwiches

BLT with spicy guacamole

Serves 4
Preparation time: 15 minutes

vegetable oil for frying
8 slices back bacon
4 bread rolls, halved
1 large tomato, thinly sliced
45 g/1½ oz rocket leaves

spicy guacamole
1 large ripe avocado
1 tablespoon finely chopped red onion
1 teaspoon finely diced red chilli
2 tablespoons roughly chopped coriander leaves
2 teaspoons lime juice
sea salt and freshly ground black pepper

For the spicy guacamole, peel the avocado, place the flesh in a bowl and lightly mash with a fork. Add the remaining ingredients to taste and mix well. For a smoother guacamole, whizz the whole lot in a food processor. Cover and set aside.

Place a large frying pan over a medium heat and add a small amount of oil to the pan. Add the bacon slices and cook for 2–3 minutes on each side or until crispy, then drain on absorbent kitchen paper.

Put the 4 bread roll bases on a board and spread each one with a layer of guacamole. Top with the tomato slices, followed by 2 slices of bacon. Finish with a handful of rocket leaves and replace the lids. Serve while the bacon is warm.

Breakfast baguette

Serves 4
Preparation time: 25 minutes

vegetable oil
4 slices back bacon
4 free-range pork chipolatas
2 tomatoes, quartered
sea salt and freshly ground black pepper
4 large free-range eggs
15 g/½ oz butter
1 baguette, or 4 long bread rolls
ketchup, to serve

A full breakfast in a roll – this one has it all. You can also use fried or poached eggs instead of scrambled.

Preheat the oven to 200°C/400°F/gas mark 6. Lightly oil a large roasting tin Place the bacon, chipolatas and tomatoes in a single layer in the tin. Season the tomatoes. Place the tin in the oven for 20 minutes, turning over the bacon and chipolatas halfway through to colour evenly.

Break the eggs into a bowl and whisk lightly. Place a non-stick frying pan over a medium heat and add the butter, swirling it around to coat the base. Pour the beaten eggs into the pan and stir gently for 2 minutes or until the eggs are just cooked through. Take off the heat and season.

Cut the baguette into 4 lengths, if using, roughly the length of the bacon slices. Split the baguette lengths or the rolls and fill with the scrambled eggs, followed by the bacon, chipolatas and tomato quarters. Dot with ketchup and serve.

Char-grilled focaccia with portabello mushrooms, pesto and Gruyère cheese

Serves 4
Preparation time: 20 minutes

300 g/11 oz large portabello mushrooms,
    cut in 1cm/½in slices
1 teaspoon thyme leaves, chopped
2 tablespoons olive oil
sea salt and freshly ground black pepper
4 x 13 cm/5 inch squares of focaccia
4 tablespoons pesto (see Pesto, pine nut and parmesan
    stuffed tomatoes recipe, page 89)
150 g/5 oz Gruyère cheese, sliced

Try adding your favourites to this tasty vegetarian sandwich. Sliced green olives, marinated artichokes and grilled vegetables, such as peppers, aubergines and courgettes work well.

Preheat a large ridged griddle pan over a high heat. Place the mushroom slices, thyme and olive oil in a bowl and toss to lightly coat the mushrooms. Season the mushrooms and put half of them on the pan, cooking for 2 minutes on each side or until they soften and colour. Transfer to a plate and repeat with the remaining mushrooms.

Cut the focaccia squares in half horizontally and smear the cut side of the 4 bases with the pesto. Top with the mushrooms and cheese then season with black pepper. Place the focaccia lids on top and transfer to the hot griddle pan, cooking for 1½–2 minutes on each side or until they are nicely marked by the grill. Serve hot or warm.

Sourdough eggy bread with maple-cured bacon and roasted vine tomatoes

Serves 4
Preparation time: 30 minutes

24 baby plum tomatoes, preferably on the vine
2 tablespoons olive oil
sea salt and freshly ground black pepper
8 slices maple or sweetcure bacon
3 large free-range eggs
2 tablespoons milk
4 thick slices sourdough bread
15 g/½ oz butter

For pesto eggy bread, try smearing the sourdough slices generously with pesto before soaking in the egg.

Preheat the oven to 180°C/350°F/gas mark 4. Put the tomatoes in a small baking dish, drizzle over the olive oil and season. Place in the oven for 25 minutes.

Lightly oil a large baking tray, then lay the bacon slices on it and cook in the oven for 15 minutes, turning the slices over halfway through.

Meanwhile, place the eggs, milk and some seasoning in a wide shallow bowl and whisk to combine. Lay the bread slices in the mixture, turn them to coat both sides and leave to soak for a few minutes, as sourdough bread can be dense.

Add most of the butter to a large non-stick frying pan set over a medium heat. Remove the soaked bread slices from the bowl and place in the pan. Cook for 1½–2 minutes or until golden brown. Turn the slices over and add the remaining butter. Cook for a further 1½–2 minutes and remove from pan.

Warm 4 plates and place a slice of eggy bread on each. Cover each piece of bread with 2 bacon slices and serve with the tomatoes and any of their cooking juices spooned over.

Char-grilled panini with proscuitto, tomato and Taleggio cheese

Serves 4
Preparation time: 10 minutes

4 panini or ciabatta rolls, halved
8 slices proscuitto
150 g/5 oz Taleggio cheese, sliced
2 ripe tomatoes, sliced
freshly ground black pepper

These Italian-inspired toasted sandwiches can also be made with mozzarella, fontina or provolone cheese. They can be assembled several hours in advance and grilled at the last minute.

Preheat a large ridged griddle pan over a high heat. Place the 4 panini bases on a board and cover each one with 2 slices of proscuitto. Place the cheese and tomato slices over the proscuitto, season with freshly ground black pepper and put the top half of the panini in place.

Place the paninis on the griddle pan and cover with a heavy frying pan to weigh them down. Cook them for 1½–2 minutes or until nicely browned, then turn over and repeat on the other side. Serve straight away so the cheese is piping hot and runny.

Mozzarella en carozza

Serves 2
Preparation time: 10 minutes

120 g/4 oz ball buffalo mozzarella cheese,
    or 2 x 60 g/2 oz slices
4 slices soft white bread
freshly ground black pepper
1 large free-range egg
2 tablespoons milk
4 teaspoons olive oil
3 anchovies in olive oil, finely chopped

Small but deliciously rich, these pan-fried mozzarella sandwiches are utterly delectable. Serve straight away so the cheese is nice and oozy.

Cut the mozzarella ball in half, pressing down on each piece with your palm to flatten it slightly. Cut the bread in rounds about 1 cm/½ inch bigger than the mozzarella slices. You can use a large round cutter to do this neatly.

Place 2 of the bread circles on a plate and top each one with a slice of mozzarella. Season with black pepper and top with another bread circle. Gently squash each sandwich together with your hands to compress them and prevent them from opening up.

Place the egg and milk in a wide shallow bowl and whisk lightly. Gently dip the sandwiches in the beaten egg, making sure they are well covered. Leave the sandwiches to soak while you put the olive oil and the anchovies in a frying pan over a medium heat.

Remove the sandwiches from the egg mix and place them in the pan. Cook for 2 minutes or until golden brown, then turn them over and repeat on the other side. The anchovies will melt in the oil and cling to the sandwiches. Remove from the pan and serve piping hot.

Foiled-baked bacon, egg
and cheese muffins

Serves 4
Preparation time: 25 minutes

vegetable oil, for brushing
4 English muffins, split in half
4 large slices back bacon
4 large free-range eggs
4 thick slices cheese, see below

Cooking these delicious parcels in foil gives the
muffins a wonderful soft and fluffy steaminess. For a
toastier effect you can do away with the foil and bake
as directed. Use any good melting cheese, such as
Comté, Emmental, Gruyère or fontina.

Preheat oven to 200°C/400°F/gas mark 6. Cut out 4 squares
of aluminium foil, large enough to generously envelope each
muffin. Lightly brush the squares with oil and place a muffin
half in the middle of each one.

Put a large non-stick frying pan over a medium heat and
brush with oil. Add the bacon rashers and cook them for
2–3 minutes on each side or until they are cooked and
slightly crispy. Remove the rashers from the pan and drain
on absorbent kitchen paper.

Wipe out the pan, return to the heat and brush with oil.
Place 4 lightly oiled egg rings in the pan and break an egg
in each one. Cook for 2 minutes, then gently remove the
rings, flip the eggs over and repeat. The yolks will not have
set completely but will carry on cooking in the oven. Place
an egg on each of the 4 muffin halves and top with the
bacon and cheese. Cover with the muffin lids and wrap
the muffins loosely in the foil squares. Place the foil packages
on a baking sheet and transfer to the oven for 8 minutes.
Remove the hot muffins from the foil and serve immediately
for maximum ooziness.

Char-grilled pitta bread with hot smoked salmon, crème fraîche and salmon caviar

Serves 4
Preparation time: 10 minutes

230 g/8 oz hot-smoked salmon, skinned
4 heaped tablespoons crème fraîche
2 tablespoons finely chopped chives
4 teaspoons salmon caviar
1 tablespoon lemon juice
freshly ground black pepper
4 pitta bread ovals
handful baby spinach leaves

This luxuriously rich sandwich calls for hot smoked salmon, which is the opaque, cooked-looking flakeable stuff sold in pieces. It has a moistness and texture that cold-smoked salmon is unable to deliver. Salmon caviar, often sold as keta or salmon eggs, is available from good food halls and supermarkets, or from fishmongers.

Preheat a large ridged griddle pan over a high heat. Roughly flake the fish into large pieces and place in a mixing bowl. Add the crème fraîche, chives, salmon caviar, lemon juice and a few grindings of black pepper. Gently fold the mixture to combine so the fish doesn't break up too much.

Split each pitta bread down one side to create a long pocket. Place a quarter of the salmon mixture inside each pocket, spreading it down to cover the bread evenly. Place a few spinach leaves on top of the filling and press down gently to close the pocket.

Place the filled breads on the griddle and cook them for 1–1½ minutes on each side. Cut each pitta in half and serve while still hot.

Baby lox and bagels

Preparation time: 10 minutes
Makes 12 (serves 6)

180 g/6 oz cream cheese
12 baby bagels, halved horizontally
250 g/9 oz oak-smoked salmon slices
freshly ground black pepper
12 sprigs dill
2 small lemons, each cut into 6 wedges
a handful of small salted capers, soaked in water
    and squeezed dry
a handful of thin red onion slices

These cute little bagels can be prepared in advance, making them ideal for a breakfast buffet. Baby bagels are available from good food halls, specialist bakers and some supermarkets. You can use regular-sized bagels and double the filling if you have trouble tracking them down. Allow 2 baby bagels per person.

Smear the cream cheese over the bagel bases and top with the smoked salmon slices. Season with black pepper and replace the bagel tops. Stack the bagels onto a platter and serve with small bowls of dill, lemon wedges, capers and onion slices.

Eggs

Soft-boiled eggs with anchovy and rosemary butter soldiers

Makes 4
Preparation time: 10 minutes

30 g/1 oz butter
2 anchovies in olive oil, very finely chopped
½ teaspoon finely chopped rosemary leaves
small squeeze lemon juice
freshly ground black pepper
4 large free-range eggs, at room temperature
4 thick slices of white bread

There is nothing like dunking super buttery toast fingers into dribbly soft-set egg yolk. Add some anchovies and rosemary to the equation and you are just about in heaven.

The anchovies in the butter add the salt that eggs cry out for. You could use sun-dried tomatoes or pesto for a vegetarian option.

Place the butter, anchovies, rosemary, lemon juice and black pepper into a small bowl and mash with a fork.

Using a tablespoon, lower the eggs, one by one, into a small pan of boiling water. Cook for 4½ minutes then remove from the water and place in egg cups.

Meanwhile, toast the bread and discard the crusts. Smear generously with the butter, cut into fingers and dunk away.

Eggs en cocotte with chorizo, peppers and smoked paprika

Makes 4
Preparation time: 45 minutes

75 g/2½ oz chorizo, peeled and cut into small cubes
1 small red pepper, deseeded and cut into thin strips
1 small red onion, sliced
1 ripe tomato, cut into 8 wedges
¼ teaspoon sweet smoked paprika
1 teaspoon olive oil, plus extra for brushing
4 large free-range eggs

These spicy baked eggs require no seasoning as the chorizo delivers the salt and spice in equally good measures. Top with a dash of Tabasco for a chilli jolt.

Preheat the oven to 200°C/400°F/gas mark 6. Toss the chorizo, peppers, onion, tomato, smoked paprika and olive oil in a bowl and transfer to a small roasting tin. Cook in the oven for 25 minutes, stirring every now and then. The mixture should be soft and stewy with slightly charred edges.

Brush 4 small ramekins with olive oil and divide the softened mixture among them. Break an egg into each ramekin and place in the cleaned roasting tin. Pour boiling water into the roasting tin to reach halfway up the sides of the ramekins. Carefully place in the oven and bake for 10 minutes or until the egg whites have just set.

Remove from the oven, transfer the ramekins to small plates and serve with chunks of warm bread for dipping.

Eggs Benedict with smoked trout

Makes 4
Preparation time: 20 minutes

hollandaise sauce
2 large free-range egg yolks
2 teaspoons lemon juice
120 g/4 oz cold butter, cubed
sea salt and cayenne pepper

1 tablespoon white wine vinegar
4 large free-range eggs
2 English muffins, each split in half
120 g/4 oz smoked trout slices
1 heaped tablespoon chopped chives
sea salt and freshly ground black pepper

The combination of gooey poached eggs, a thick buttery sauce and lightly smoked fish is rarely equalled. Oak-smoked salmon will work just as well here as the trout.

If the sauce needs to be re-warmed you can place the topped muffins under the grill for a few minutes and serve with the sauce lightly bubbling. Garnish with the chives just before serving.

To make the hollandaise sauce, place the egg yolks and lemon juice in a double boiler or heatproof bowl set over a pan of barely simmering water. Make sure that the base of the bowl does not actually touch the simmering water. Whisk or stir until the mixture thickens, then add a cube of the cold butter and whisk or stir until it is combined. Continue with the butter cubes, a few at a time, until they are incorporated and the sauce is thick and glossy. Take the pan off the heat and season with salt and a pinch of cayenne pepper. Leave the bowl of sauce on top of the pan to keep warm while you prepare the eggs.

Put a wide, shallow pan over a medium heat and add a few inches of water. Add the white wine vinegar and bring to a gentle simmer. Break an egg into a small cup and gently slide it into the hot water. Repeat with 3 more eggs. Cook for 4 minutes then remove the eggs with a slotted spoon and place on absorbent kitchen paper.

Meanwhile, toast or grill the muffin halves and transfer to a warmed platter. Drape the smoked trout slices over the muffins and top each one with a poached egg. Spoon one or two heaped tablespoons of hollandaise sauce over each egg, sprinkle with the chopped chives and serve.

Eggs Florentine on toasted sourdough

Makes 4
Preparation time: 30 minutes

cheese sauce
15 g/½ oz butter
1½ teaspoons plain flour
150 ml/5 fl oz milk, warmed
30 g/1 oz grated Parmesan cheese, plus an extra 15 g/½ oz
  for grilling
a few fresh grindings of whole nutmeg
sea salt and freshly ground black pepper

120 g/4 oz tender spinach leaves, washed and well dried
1 tablespoon white wine vinegar
4 large free-range eggs
4 small thick slices sourdough bread

A nutmeg-spiced Parmesan cheese sauce transforms spinach and eggs into something truly special. For a lighter breakfast, you can transfer the lot to a heatproof serving dish and do away with the bread.

To make the cheese sauce, melt the butter in a small pan over a low heat and add the flour. Whisk or stir until smooth then cook for a minute, stirring often. Add a splash of the warmed milk, then whisk or stir until it is incorporated. Add the remaining milk in small batches, whisking or stirring between each addition. If you add too much milk at once the sauce tends to go lumpy. Keep whisking or stirring until the mixture starts to thicken then add the cheese. Continue stirring until the cheese melts and the sauce is smooth. Cook for a further minute or until the sauce is nice and thick. Season with nutmeg, salt and pepper and set aside.

Place a large pan over a high heat and add the spinach. Cook for a minute until the leaves are soft and wilted then season and transfer to a plate. Cover with foil to keep warm and set aside until needed.

Preheat the grill to medium. Place a wide, shallow pan over a medium heat and add a few inches of water. Add the white wine vinegar and bring to a gentle simmer. Break an egg into a small cup and gently slide into the hot water. Repeat with 3 more eggs. Cook for 4 minutes then remove with a slotted spoon and place on absorbent kitchen paper.

Lightly toast or grill the bread slices and place on a baking sheet. Divide the spinach among the 4 pieces of toast and top each one with a poached egg. Spoon a quarter of the sauce over each egg. The sauce thickens as it cools, so if it is too thick you can whisk in a splash of milk to let it down. Scatter the remaining cheese over the sauce and place under the grill for a few minutes until the cheese is nicely browned. Transfer to warmed plates and serve.

Scrambled duck eggs with crème fraîche and caviar

Serves 2–4
Preparation time: 10 minutes

4 duck eggs
15 g/½ oz butter
1 tablespoon soured cream or crème fraîche
2 teaspoons finely chopped chives
sea salt and freshly ground black pepper
2 teaspoons caviar

The duck eggs' incredibly rich yolk makes these scrambled eggs sublime. Buy the best caviar you can afford – or herring roe at a push. Serve piping hot with buttery toast fingers.

The eggs look lovely served in their shells but for less of a fiddle you can simply spoon the mixture onto slices of hot buttered toast.

Crack the eggs towards the top so that you are left with most of the shell intact. Discard the top piece of broken shell then gently pick off any excess shell fragments. Tip the eggs into a mixing bowl then carefully rinse and wipe the inside of the shells clean. Cut or tear an egg carton so that you have 4 little bases to hold the egg shells.

Whisk the eggs and place the butter in a non-stick pan set over a medium heat. Swirl the butter around the pan and add the beaten eggs. Gently stir for 1½–2 minutes or until the eggs are almost cooked through. They will carry on cooking after they come off the heat. Take off the heat, stir in crème fraîche and chives and season lightly. Spoon the scrambled eggs back into the reserved eggshells. Serve any left over separately. Top with the caviar, place in the egg carton bases and serve with small teaspoons.

Oak-smoked salmon and chive scrambled eggs on toasted brioche

Serves 2
Preparation time: 10 minutes

2 thick slices of brioche
4 large free-range eggs
freshly ground black pepper
15 g/½ oz butter
60 g/2 oz oak-smoked salmon, chopped
2 tablespoons double cream
1 tablespoon finely chopped chives

Rich and delightful, these creamy, buttery eggs work so well with the subtle yeastiness of toasted brioche. Avoid over-sweet brioche – you don't want to overpower the eggs.

Grill or toast the brioche slices and keep warm. Meanwhile, break the eggs into a bowl, season with black pepper and whisk lightly. Place the butter into a non-stick frying pan set over a medium heat and swirl it around to coat the base. Pour in the eggs and stir gently for 1½ minutes then add the salmon and cream and cook for up to half a minute, stirring constantly until the mixture is almost cooked through. The eggs will carry on cooking after they come off the heat. Stir in the chives and take off the heat. Place the toasted brioche on 2 plates, top with the creamy eggs and serve straight away.

Bacon-wrapped baked eggs

Makes 6
Preparation time: 20 minutes

olive oil for brushing
9 slices streaky bacon, not too fatty
6 medium free-range eggs
6 small cherry tomatoes, halved
2 tablespoons soured cream
sea salt and freshly ground black pepper

These hand-held breakfast bundles work just as well as a picnic dish as they are easy to eat and can be served at room temperature. Make sure the bacon is relatively lean and look for long even slices if possible.

Preheat the oven to 200°C/400°F/gas mark 6. Lightly brush a non-stick 6-cup muffin tin with olive oil and wrap a piece of bacon around the inside of each cup. Cut the remaining bacon slices in half and place a piece in each of the holes to line the bases. Break an egg into each cup and top with 2 cherry tomato halves. Place a teaspoon of soured cream on top of each one, season lightly and cook in the oven for 12 minutes or until the egg whites are just set.

Run a small knife around the edges to loosen the wrapped eggs and transfer them to a serving plate. Eat hot, warm or at room temperature.

Free-range sausage, roasted tomato and pecorino frittata

Serves 4
Preparation time: 30 minutes, plus tomato cooking time

1 tablespoon olive oil
250 g/9 oz thin free-range pork sausages
6 large free-range eggs
30 g/1 oz pecorino cheese, grated
1 tablespoon chopped oregano
freshly ground black pepper
1 quantity Thyme-scented slow-roasted tomatoes
  (see page 89), or 8 cooked tomato halves, cooled

This one-stop breakfast dish is easily adaptable to make use of leftovers. Try cooked bacon, mushrooms, ham or potato if you have any hanging around.

Heat 1 teaspoon of the olive oil into a frying pan placed over a medium high heat. Add the sausages and cook, turning frequently, for 7 minutes or until they are cooked through and nicely coloured. Cut the sausages in half, transfer to a plate, and set aside to cool.

Preheat the grill to medium. Break the eggs into a mixing bowl, add the cheese and oregano and season with black pepper. Whisk to combine then add the sausages and tomatoes and mix again. Heat a 23 cm/9 inch non-stick frying pan over a low heat and add the remaining oil. Swirl around the pan to coat the base and pour in the egg mixture. Rearrange the top to distribute the tomatoes and sausages evenly if necessary. Cook for 10 minutes or until the sides set and the middle is still wobbly. Take off the heat and place under the grill for 5 minutes or until the middle is just set. Loosen the edges with a palette knife and gently slide onto a serving plate. Serve hot or warm.

Feta, sunblush tomato and basil soufflé omelette

Serves 2
Preparation time: 15 minutes

60 g/2 oz feta cheese, crumbled
45 g/1½ oz sunblush tomatoes, chopped
2 tablespoons chopped basil leaves,
    plus a few whole leaves to serve
4 large free-range eggs, separated
freshly ground black pepper
1 heaped teaspoon butter

The punchy flavours of feta, sunblush tomatoes and basil work beautifully in this light and fluffy soufflé omelette. Sunblush tomatoes are intensely flavoured, slow-cooked tomatoes in a herb infused oil. They are usually available by weight at deli counters.

Preheat the grill to medium high. Add about two-thirds of the cheese, and the tomatoes and chopped basil to the egg yolks. Season well with pepper and stir to combine.

Heat a 23 cm/9 inch non-stick frying pan over a medium heat. Whisk the eggs whites with an electric whisk until soft peaks form. Gently fold the beaten egg whites into the yolk mixture without overworking them – you need to retain as much air as possible.

Add the butter to the pan, swirl it around to coat the base and pour in the omelette mixture. Cook for 2 minutes then take off the heat. Scatter the remaining cheese over the omelette and place under the grill, a few inches away from the element; if it is too close the top of the omelette will brown whilst the middle will remain uncooked.

Cook for 4 minutes or until the top is golden and bubbling. Loosen the omelette with a palette knife and gently fold in half. Slide onto a warmed plate, top with the whole basil leaves and eat straight away.

Spanish omelette with char-grilled tomato bread

Serves 4
Preparation time: 50 minutes

350 g/12 oz small waxy potatoes
1 large onion, sliced
4 tablespoons olive oil
sea salt and freshly ground black pepper
5 large free-range eggs

Unlike many egg dishes, Spanish omelette, or tortilla española, is even better when served slightly warm or at room temperature. It needs more seasoning than you think, so don't be afraid of being heavy handed. Serve on its own or with slices or char-grilled tomato bread (see opposite).

Slice the potatoes into 3 mm/⅒ inch rounds and place them in a mixing bowl. Add the onion slices and olive oil and stir well to coat. Heat a large non-stick frying pan over a medium to low heat and tip in the potato mixture. If you don't have a pan big enough you can use 2 smaller ones. Cook, stirring every now and then, for 30 minutes or until the potatoes and onions are meltingly tender and lightly coloured. Turn down the heat if it the mixture colours too much at any stage during the cooking. Use a slotted spoon to transfer the potatoes and onions to a plate and season generously. Reserve a tablespoon of the cooking oil and discard the rest.

Break the eggs into a bowl, season well and beat lightly. Place a 23 cm/9 inch non-stick frying pan over a low heat and add the reserved oil. Swirl the oil around to coat the base and sides of the pan. Add the cooked potatoes and onions to the pan then pour the beaten eggs on top. Cook for

8 minutes, using a blunt knife to make small indents in the base to allow the liquidy egg to run into. The base should be set and the middle still a little runny. Invert a large plate over the pan and gently but swiftly turn it upside down so that the cooked side is facing upwards. Gently slide the omelette back into the pan and press down with a spatula to reshape if necessary. Cook for 2 minutes or until the eggs are just set. Take off the heat, turn onto a plate and allow the omelette to cool for at least 5 minutes. Cut into wedges and serve warm or at room temperature with the char-grilled tomato bread.

Char-grilled tomato bread

Serves 4
Preparation time: 5 minutes

4 thick slices of day-old rustic bread –
    something dense and chewy is perfect
1 small clove garlic, peeled (optional)
1 very ripe tomato, halved
extra virgin olive oil
sea salt and freshly ground black pepper

Char-grilled tomato bread, or *pa amb tomàquet*, is a Catalan speciality. Although it's not the traditional accompaniment to tortilla it does work well as an optional extra.

Preheat a ridged griddle pan over a high heat. Place the bread slices on the pan, cooking for a minute on each side or until nicely charred on the edges. Transfer the bread to a large plate and lightly rub each slice with the garlic, if using. Squeeze the tomato halves over each piece of bread, rubbing the cut side into the bread so that it absorbs some of the flesh and seeds. Drizzle each bread slice with olive oil, season and serve warm or at room temperature.

Breton buckwheat crêpes with ham, eggs and Gruyère

Serves 6
Preparation time: 50 minutes, plus 1 hour for the batter to rest

crêpes
120 g/4 oz buckwheat flour
1 large egg
¼ teaspoon salt
250 ml/9 fl oz water
15 g/½ oz melted butter, plus extra butter for cooking

filling
6 free-range eggs
170 g/6 oz Gruyère cheese, grated
6 slices ham, cut or torn into strips
sea salt and freshly ground black pepper
2 tablespoons crème fraîche, optional

Known as galettes in their native Brittany, these crêpes have a distinctively deep savouriness brought on by the buckwheat flour. You could replace the ham with spinach for a vegetarian version.

If you happen to have 2 pans you can halve the cooking time by making 2 crêpes at once.

Place the buckwheat flour, egg and salt in a blender with 250 ml/9 fl oz water and mix until smooth. Transfer to a mixing bowl and leave to rest for at least 1 hour and up to overnight. Then pour in the melted butter and 5 tablespoons water and whisk until the batter is thin and smooth.

Heat a large non-stick frying pan (I use a 29 cm/11½ inch one) over a medium heat and add a small knob of butter, swirling it around to lightly coat the base. Stir the batter and quickly pour in enough to lightly cover the base, swirling it around to get a thin lacy crêpe. Swiftly tip any excess batter away. If you aren't quick enough the excess batter will cook and the crêpe will be too thick. Break an egg into the middle of the crêpe and gently swirl the egg white around the crepe to allow it to spread and cook faster. Once the egg white begins to turn opaque carefully reposition the yolk to the middle if it has moved. Scatter the cheese and ham around the crêpe but not on the egg yolk. Season and allow the crêpe to cook for 4 minutes or until the egg white is completely cooked and the crêpe is golden and crispy underneath. Fold the crêpe into a square by folding 4 edges inwards so that only the egg yolk peeks through. Transfer to a warmed plate, top with a dollop of crème fraîche, if using, and serve. Repeat with the remaining mixture to make five more crêpes, serving each one as soon as it is ready so that it retains its slightly crispy texture.

Brunch

Fried green tomatoes with spicy bacon and red pepper cornbread

Serves 8
Preparation time: 1 hour 20 minutes

cornbread
1 tablespoon olive oil plus extra for oiling
120 g/4 oz smoked bacon, chopped
1 red pepper, trimmed and finely diced
1 red chilli, finely chopped
150 ml/5 fl oz milk
150 g/5 oz yoghurt
60 g/2 oz butter, melted
2 large free-range eggs
250 g/9 oz cornmeal
150 g/5 oz plain flour
2 teaspoons baking powder
1 teaspoon bicarbonate of soda
½ teaspoon fine sea salt
½ teaspoon cayenne pepper
pinch sugar
90 g/3 oz red Leicester cheese, diced

tomatoes
vegetable oil for shallow frying
250 g/9 oz cornmeal
8 green tomatoes
sea salt and freshly ground black pepper

If you haven't got any red Leicester cheese try substituting a tasty Cheddar instead.

For the cornbread, preheat oven to 180°C/350°F/gas mark 4. Lightly oil and line a 25 cm/10 inch square cake tin. Place the olive oil in a frying pan set over medium heat. Add the bacon, red pepper and chilli and cook for 5 minutes, stirring regularly. Tip out into a bowl and set aside.

Place the milk, yoghurt, butter and eggs in a large mixing bowl and whisk to combine. Sift the dry ingredients together and fold into the liquid. Then fold in the bacon, red pepper, chilli and cheese. Spoon the batter into the prepared tin, smoothing over the top with a wet spoon. Place in the oven for 25 minutes or until a skewer inserted in the cornbread comes out clean. Set aside to cool slightly while you prepare the tomatoes.

Place a large frying pan over a medium high heat and add enough vegetable oil for shallow frying. Spread the cornmeal in a wide shallow bowl. Slice each tomato across in 4 thick slices. Lay the slices out on a large board and season well. Dip the tomato slices in the cornmeal, shake to remove any excess then gently slide enough tomato slices to fit snugly in a single layer in the hot oil. Cook for 3–4 minutes or until golden then gently turn over and repeat on the other side. Remove from the pan and place on absorbent kitchen paper to drain. Keep the cooked tomatoes warm. Wipe out the pan if necessary and repeat with the remaining tomatoes. You should be able to cook them in 3 batches. Serve the hot tomatoes with squares of warm cornbread.

Spicy corn fritters with salsa

Serves 4
Preparation time: 30 minutes

3 corn cobs, husks removed
1 fat spring onion, thinly sliced
1 heaped teaspoon finely diced red chilli
2 tablespoons chopped coriander leaves
2 tablespoons milk
1 large free-range egg, separated
¼ teaspoon smoked paprika
2 tablespoons plain flour
½ teaspoon baking powder
fine sea salt
vegetable oil, for shallow frying
soured cream, to serve

salsa
2 tomatoes, deseeded and diced
1 ripe avocado, peeled and flesh cubed
2 teaspoons lime juice
1 tablespoon chopped coriander leaves
1 teaspoon finely diced red chilli
sea salt and freshly ground black pepper

Place all the salsa ingredients in a bowl and stir. Taste and adjust the flavours to your liking. Cover and set aside.

For the corn fritters, use a sharp knife to cut the corn kernels off the cob. You will need about 200 g/7 oz. Place the corn kernels, spring onion, chilli, coriander, milk and egg yolk in a large mixing bowl. Mix the paprika, flour and baking powder together and stir into the corn mixture. Add a generous sprinkling of salt and stir to combine.

Place the egg white in a mixing bowl and beat until stiff. Gently fold the beaten white into the corn mixture.

Use 2 heaped tablespoons of batter per fritter and shallow-fry in hot oil, 4 at a time in a large pan. Fry them for 1½–2 minutes or until golden brown. Gently turn over with a spatula and cook the other side. Drain on absorbent kitchen paper. You should be able to make 8 fritters. Serve hot topped with salsa and soured cream.

Mushrooms on toast

Serves 4
Preparation time: 15 minutes

45 g/1½ oz butter, plus extra for the toast
300 g/11 oz wild or cultivated mushrooms, cleaned and quartered
1 heaped tablespoon chopped flat-leaf parsley
sea salt and freshly ground black pepper
4 thick slices white bread
a few drops of truffle oil, to serve (optional)

You can use wild or cultivated mushrooms for this wonderfully fragrant version of mushrooms on toast. The truffle oil is extremely strong, so be sparing.

Melt the butter in a large frying pan placed over a high heat. Add the mushrooms and cook for 4 minutes or until they soften and colour nicely. Take off the heat, add the parsley and season well.

Toast the bread and butter each piece generously. Pile the mushrooms on the hot buttered toast, top with few drops of truffle oil, if using, and serve.

Smoked salmon hash

Serves 4
Preparation time: 45 minutes

600 g/1 lb 5 oz all-purpose potatoes, peeled and
  halved or quartered
3 tablespoons olive oil
1 small red pepper, finely diced
1 small red onion, finely sliced
200 g/7 oz hot-smoked salmon fillet,
  skinned and flaked into large chunks
1½ tablespoons chopped dill
1½ tablespoons small salted capers,
  soaked in water and squeezed dry
sea salt and cayenne pepper
4 lemon wedges, to serve
soured cream, to serve (optional)

This dish requires hot-smoked salmon fillets – the
ones sold in pieces that are flaked rather than sliced.
They have a wonderfully mild smoky flavour and oily
rich texture that complements the punchy flavours of
this hash. Top with a fried or poached egg for a
substantial brunch dish.

Boil the potatoes in a large pan of salted water until tender.
Drain in a colander and set aside to cool while you prepare
the peppers and onions.
  Pour a tablespoon of oil into a large non-stick frying pan
set over a medium low heat. Add the peppers and onion and
cook for 7 minutes or until they soften. Transfer to a plate
and set aside.
  Cut the cooked potatoes into large dice. Place the frying
pan over a medium heat and add the rest of the oil. Add
the diced potatoes and cook for 8 minutes or until nicely
browned and crispy. Add the softened peppers and onion and
cook for a few more minutes until they begin to crisp at the
edges. Take off the heat and fold in the salmon, dill and
capers. Season with sea salt and cayenne pepper and transfer
to 4 warmed plates. Serve with lemon wedges and top with
a dollop of soured cream, if using.

Grilled Craster kippers with lemon and chive butter

Serves 4
Preparation time: 10 minutes

30 g/1 oz soft butter
½ teaspoon finely grated lemon zest
1 teaspoon finely chopped chives
1 teaspoon lemon juice
large pinch cayenne pepper
4 x 180 g/6 oz Craster kippers
4 lemon wedges
brown toast, to serve

Craster kippers are oak-smoked herrings sold as
whole split fish. If you are not fond of bones you can
often buy the fillets in attached pairs. As kippers are
rather salty, lemon juice is a must.

Preheat the grill to medium. Place the butter, lemon zest,
chives, lemon juice and cayenne pepper in a small bowl and
mix to combine.
  Lay the kippers skin side up on a lightly oiled baking tray.
Set under the grill for 2 minutes then remove and turn the
kippers over. Dot with the butter and place back under the
grill for 2 minutes or until the fish has warmed through.
  Place the kippers, flesh side up, on a warmed serving
platter and pour any excess butter on top. Serve with lemon
wedges and lots of hot brown toast.

Kedgeree risotto cakes with poached eggs

Serves 6
Preparation time: 1 hour 20 minutes, plus 1 hour cooling time

300 g/11 oz smoked haddock fillet, with skin on
1 bay leaf
300 ml/11 fl oz chicken stock
30 g/1 oz butter
1 onion, finely chopped
200 g/7 oz arborio rice
1½ teaspoons mild to medium curry powder
75 g/2½ oz frozen peas, thawed
1½ tablespoons chopped flat-leaf parsley
1½ tablespoons chopped coriander
1 tablespoon lemon juice
vegetable oil, for shallow frying
6 poached eggs (see poached eggs page 93)
6 lemon wedges, to serve

This take on kedgeree transforms it in an elegant brunch dish. Ditching hard-boiled eggs in favour of soft-poached ones gives these crisp-edged cakes their own silky sauce. To save time on the day you can prepare the risotto the night before.

Place the fish and bay leaf in a pan and cover with 300 ml/11 fl oz cold water. Set over a high heat and bring to the boil. Cover the pan, reduce the heat to low and cook for 8 minutes or until the fish is cooked through. Remove the fish and set aside to cool on a plate. Add the chicken stock to the fishy water, keeping the bay leaf, and leave over a low heat. This will be the stock that the risotto will cook in.

Place the butter in a heavy-based saucepan over a medium to low heat. Add the onion and cook for 7 minutes or until is softens completely without colouring. Turn up the heat, add the rice and curry powder to the pan and stir for 1 minute. Pour a ladleful of the warm stock into the pan and stir until it is absorbed into the rice. Continue ladle by ladle until the stock is absorbed and the rice is cooked but maintains a slight bite – it shouldn't be mushy. This will take about 20 minutes. Turn down the heat if the rice bubbles too much or begins to stick to the pan. Remove from the heat and discard the bay leaf.

Use your hands to peel the skin off the cooked fish and discard any bones. Flake the fish in large chunks and add it to the risotto, along with the peas, herbs and lemon juice. Gently fold the mixture to combine without breaking up the fish too much. Transfer the risotto to a large shallow dish to cool quickly. Once cool, place the risotto in the fridge for 1 hour to firm up, so that it is easier to handle.

Shape the risotto into 6 large cakes, weighing about 150 g/5 oz each. For a neater a result you can form the cakes using a 9 cm/3½ inch round cutter.

Place a non-stick frying pan over a medium heat and add enough oil to shallow fry in. Place 3 or 4 risotto cakes in the pan and cook for 5 minutes on each side or until browned. Transfer to absorbent kitchen paper to drain. Keep each batch warm while you cook the remaining cakes.

Transfer all the cooked cakes to a large warmed platter and top each one with a poached egg. Serve immediately with lemon wedges.

Lightly spiced crab cakes

Serves 4
Preparation time: 30 minutes, plus 30 minutes
chilling time

2 teaspoons lime juice
1 teaspoon finely grated lime zest
1 large free-range egg
2 tablespoons best quality mayonnaise
1 tablespoon finely chopped chives
1 tablespoon finely chopped coriander
45 g/1½ oz water biscuits, crushed to crumbs
400 g/14 oz fresh white crab meat
sea salt and freshly ground black pepper
few drops Tabasco sauce
vegetable oil, for shallow frying
4 lime wedges
45 g/1½ oz rocket leaves

This luxurious brunch dish has a mild hint of fresh
Oriental flavours. Try serving with mayonnaise mixed
with lime juice, coriander or Tabasco.

Place the lime juice, zest, egg, mayonnaise, chives and
coriander in a mixing bowl and whisk to combine. Fold in
the water-biscuit crumbs and crab meat and season with salt,
pepper and Tabasco sauce.

   Form the mixture into 8 small cakes, each weighing a little
over 60 g/2 oz. For a neater result, try forming each cake by
packing the mixture into a 7.5 cm/3 inch round cutter,
pressing down with your fingers to compact it. Use a palette
knife to transfer the cakes onto a flat tray then cover and
place in the fridge for 30 minutes. The chilling will allow
the cakes to firm up a bit, as the mixture is very delicate.

   Place a large frying pan over a medium heat and add
enough oil for shallow frying. Put 4 of the crab cakes in the
hot oil, cooking for 2½–3 minutes on each side or until
golden brown. Transfer to absorbent kitchen paper to drain
and keep warm. Repeat with the last 4 crab cakes. Serve with
lime wedges and rocket leaves.

Red flannel hash

Serves 4
Preparation time: 45 minutes

3 tablespoons vegetable oil
1 onion, finely chopped
1 stalk celery, finely diced
150 g/5 oz cooked salt beef or corned beef,
   shredded or chopped
400 g/14 oz boiled floury potatoes, diced
120 g/4 oz cooked beetroot, peeled and cubed
½ teaspoon Worcestershire sauce
sea salt and freshly ground black pepper
4 poached eggs, (see poached eggs page 93)
2 tablespoons chopped flat-leaf parsley
Dijon mustard or ketchup, to serve

Apart from its delightfully curious name, this purply-
pink mess tastes great. With its crispy edges, the
salty beef complements the sweet earthiness of the
beetroot. The addition of a soft poached eggs takes
the flavours to new heights.

Place a tablespoon of oil in a non-stick frying pan set over
a medium low heat. Add the onion and celery and cook for
10 minutes or until softened. Tip into a large mixing bowl.
Add the beef, potatoes and beetroot to the softened
vegetables. Sprinkle in the Worcestershire sauce and some
seasoning, and stir to combine.

   Wipe out the frying pan and place over a medium heat.
Add the remaining oil to the pan and swirl it around to coat
the base. Tip the potato mixture into the hot oil, pressing it
down with a wooden spoon to compact it. Cook for
10 minutes or until the base is golden and crusty. Use a fish
slice or spatula to gently turn the hash over in sections and
cook for a further 10 minutes or until the base is golden.

   Place the hash on 4 warmed plates and top with a poached
egg. Sprinkle with the chopped parsley and eat straight away
with a good dollop of mustard or ketchup.

On the side

Sticky pancetta-wrapped pork sausages with honey and mustard

Serves 4
Preparation time: 30 minutes

12 thin slices pancetta
12 thin free-range or organic pork sausages
freshly ground black pepper
2 tablespoons mustard
2 teaspoons honey

These sticky glazed sausages are easy to prepare and transform the humblest sausage into a glossy taste sensation. Serve as part of a breakfast buffet, or place in a soft white roll with a dollop of tomato ketchup.

Preheat the oven to 200°C/400°F/gas mark 6. Tightly wrap a pancetta slice around each sausage and place in a lightly oiled roasting tin. Season with pepper and place in the oven for 20 minutes, gently turning the sausages during cooking so that they colour evenly.

Mix the mustard and honey together and add to the pan with the sausages. Turn the sausages to coat them in the mixture and return to the oven for 7 minutes or until they are sticky and well coloured. Serve hot or warm.

Bubble and squeak

Makes 6
Preparation time: 25 minutes

30 g/1 oz butter
1 onion, finely chopped
450 g/1 lb cooked potatoes, roughly chopped
150 g/5 oz cooked spring greens or dark cabbage, shredded
salt and freshly ground black pepper
groundnut or olive oil for shallow frying

Named after the sound it makes when it splutters in the pan, bubble and squeak was invented to make use of roast dinner leftovers. Ironically, it is also great as a roast dinner accompaniment.

Heat the butter in a frying pan set over a medium low heat. Add the onion, cook for 7 minutes or until softened, then set aside to cool.

Place the potatoes and greens in a mixing bowl and add the softened onions. Season generously and stir to combine. Form into 6 cakes with your hands, compacting the mixture well to prevent it falling apart. You can achieve a neater look by forming the cakes in a large round cutter.

Put a large frying pan over a medium heat. Add the oil and fry the bubble and squeak cakes for a few minutes on each side or until they are golden and brown. Drain on absorbent kitchen paper and serve piping hot.

Hash browns

Makes 6
Preparation time: 40 minutes

600 g/1 lb 5 oz all-purpose potatoes, peeled and halved
15 g/½ oz butter
1 small onion, finely chopped
1½ teaspoons lemon thyme leaves, chopped
sea salt and freshly ground black pepper
olive or groundnut oil for shallow frying

Boil the potatoes in a pan of boiling salted water until they are just tender. If they are too soft, they will be difficult to grate later. Drain in a colander and leave the potatoes to cool while you prepare the onions.

Heat the butter in a frying pan set over a medium to low heat and add the onion and thyme. Cook for 8 minutes or until the onions are soft but not coloured. Take off the heat and set aside.

Once the potatoes are cool enough to handle, coarsely grate them into a large mixing bowl and add the softened onions. Season generously and mix to combine.

Heat the oil in a wide frying pan set over a medium heat. Divide the potato mixture into six and form into neat potato cakes. Fry in the oil for a few minutes on each side or until they are nicely browned and crisp at the edges. Drain on absorbent kitchen paper and serve hot.

Spicy home fries

Serves 4–6 as an accompaniment
Preparation time: 40 minutes

500 g/1 lb 2 oz small new potatoes
2 tablespoons olive oil
1 red onion, thinly sliced
1 small red pepper, diced
½ teaspoon sweet smoked paprika
sea salt and cayenne pepper

This standard diner fare is lifted to new heights with the sweetness of red onion and the spicy smokiness of cayenne pepper and smoked paprika. Serve with spicy sausages or as accompaniment to a fry up.

Boil the potatoes in a pan of salted water until just tender. Drain in a colander, allow to cool, then quarter, or halve them if they are very small.

Heat 1 tablespoon of oil in a large, preferably non-stick, frying pan over a medium heat and add the potato pieces. Cook for 10 minutes, stirring often until nicely golden. Transfer the potatoes to a plate and add the remaining oil to the pan along with the onion slices. Cook for 7 minutes, then add the diced pepper and cook for a few more minutes, stirring often until the pepper softens and the mixture browns at the edges. Return the potatoes to the pan then stir in the smoked paprika, and salt and cayenne pepper to taste. Cook for a few more minutes before transferring to a serving plate. Eat hot or warm.

Home-made baked beans

Serves 6
Preparation time: 2 hours, plus 8 hours soaking time

300 g/11 oz dried butter beans
3 tablespoons olive oil
1 onion, finely chopped
1 fat garlic clove, chopped
250 g/9 oz Italian canned chopped tomatoes
1 tablespoon double concentrate tomato purée
2 teaspoons sugar
1 tablespoon balsamic vinegar
1 bay leaf
1 large sprig of rosemary
2 bushy sprigs of thyme
sea salt and freshly ground black pepper

Although great with a fry up, these aromatic baked beans can stand up to being the star of the show. Try serving them on olive-oil-brushed toast with some crumbled feta cheese and a sprinkling of chopped parsley or dill.

The cooking time for butter beans tends to vary wildly depending on the size, variety and age of the beans. If you have a choice, go for the smaller ones and make sure they are completely cooked through before you bake them.

Place the beans in a large mixing bowl, cover with cold water and leave to soak overnight.

Drain and rinse the beans then place in a large saucepan. Cover generously with cold water and set over a high heat. Bring to the boil and remove any scum and bean skins that rise to the surface. Turn down the heat and simmer the beans for 30 minutes or until soft, regularly skimming off the foamy scum on the surface. Some larger butter beans may need up to an hour to cook. Drain the beans in a colander and reserve 200 ml/7 fl oz of the cooking water.

Preheat the oven to 160°C/325°F/gas mark 3. Place the olive oil in a flameproof casserole set over a medium heat. Add the onion and cook for 5 minutes then add the garlic and cook for a further 3 minutes or until the mixture softens completely without colouring. Add the remaining ingredients along with the beans and the reserved cooking water, stir to combine and bring to a simmer. Put the uncovered casserole in the oven for 1 hour, gently stirring every now and then. Remove from the oven, taste and add more seasoning if necessary. Serve hot or warm.

Pesto, pine nut and Parmesan-stuffed tomatoes

Makes 6
Preparation time: 30 minutes plus 5 minutes
to make the pesto

6 ripe tomatoes
olive oil
30g/1oz fresh coarse breadcrumbs
75g/2½oz fresh pesto (see recipe below)
1 tablespoon toasted pine nuts, plus a few more for serving
30g/1oz Parmesan cheese, roughly grated
sea salt and freshly ground black pepper

Preheat the oven to 190°C/370°F/gas mark 5. Cut the tops off the tomatoes and reserve. Scoop out the tomato seeds using a teaspoon. Brush the outside of the bases and the tops with oil and place the bases, cut-side up, in a lightly oiled roasting tin.

   Place the breadcrumbs, pesto and pine nuts in a bowl with half of the cheese and mix together. Add enough oil to moisten then lightly season and stuff the mixture into the 6 tomatoes. Sprinkle with the remaining cheese and bake for 15 minutes. Place the tomato lids on the bases and cook for a further 5 minutes or until they just soften. Scatter with the remaining pine nuts and serve hot or warm.

Pesto

Makes 225 g/8 oz
Preparation time: 5 minutes

45 g/1½ oz basil leaves, washed and dried
4 heaped tablespoons pine nuts, toasted and cooled
45 g/1½ oz Parmesan cheese, grated
1 small garlic clove, roughly chopped
6 tablespoons olive oil
sea salt and freshly ground black pepper

Place all the ingredients in a small food processor and whizz until you have a thick paste. Taste and adjust the seasoning. Store, covered by a layer of olive oil, in an airtight jar.

Thyme-scented slow roasted tomatoes

Serves 4
Preparation time: 3 hours 5 minutes

4 ripe plum tomatoes, halved lengthways
½ small clove garlic, thinly sliced (optional)
1 heaped teaspoon thyme leaves
2 tablespoons olive oil
sea salt flakes and freshly ground black pepper

A long, slow roasting gives these tomatoes an intense flavour and aroma. They are sweet, sticky and irresistibly squidgy, making them a versatile ingredient in sandwiches, salads and pasta dishes. You can use any well-flavoured tomato, and the recipe can be multiplied as long as the tomatoes are cooked in a single layer.

Preheat the oven to 110°C/225°F/ gas mark ½. Arrange the tomatoes cut side up in a single layer in a small baking dish. Scatter the garlic slices, if using, and the thyme over the tomatoes and drizzle with the olive oil. Season well and roast in the oven for 3 hours or until they look slightly wrinkled on the outside whilst being juicy inside. Serve hot, warm or at room temperature.

Sautéed portabello mushrooms with garlic and thyme

Serves 4 as a side dish
Preparation time: 10 minutes

30 g/1 oz butter
1 tablespoon olive oil
300 g/11 oz portabello mushrooms, sliced
1 clove garlic, lightly crushed
1 teaspoon thyme leaves, chopped
sea salt and freshly ground black pepper

As well as being great on their own, these scrumptious mushrooms are a welcome addition to any fry up. The garlic is removed after cooking, leaving behind a mild flavour. If that is too much at breakfast time it can be omitted. Instead of portabello mushrooms, you can substitute any cultivated mushrooms you have handy.

Place a large frying pan over a medium to high heat and add the butter and oil. When hot, add the mushroom slices, garlic and thyme and cook for 7 minutes, stirring often until the mushrooms are nicely coloured and free of excess moisture. Remove from the heat, discard the garlic clove and season the mushrooms well. Serve hot or warm.

Sautéed spinach

Serves 4
Preparation time: 3 minutes

15 g/½ oz butter
250 g/9 oz small spinach leaves, washed and well dried
few gratings fresh nutmeg
sea salt and freshly ground black pepper

Spinach should be cooked quickly to retain its freshness and prevent it becoming a soggy mass. This spinach is cooked for one minute, just long enough to shake off its raw crunch. You can replace the butter with a tablespoon of olive oil for a dairy-free version.

Place a large saucepan over the highest possible heat and add the butter, stirring it around to cover the base. Add the spinach and stir briskly for 1 minute until just cooked. Season with nutmeg, salt and pepper and serve at once.

Warm yoghurt breakfast scones

Makes 10
Preparation time: 25 minutes

250 g/9 oz plain flour, plus a little extra
3 teaspoons baking powder
¼ teaspoon fine sea salt
90 g/3 oz cold butter, cubed
180 g/6 oz yoghurt

These puffed-up breakfast treats are a cross between a scone and an American breakfast biscuit. Eaten piping hot, they are served in place of bread with savoury breakfasts. They have a crispy base with a light fluffy middle, making them ideal for mopping up beans, roasted tomato juices or runny yolks. You could also try topping then with some smoked salmon, crème fraîche and a sprinkling of chopped dill.

Preheat the oven to 230°C/450°F/gas mark 8. Sift the flour, baking powder and sea salt into a large mixing bowl. Add the butter and work it into the flour using your fingertips or a butter knife until the mixture resembles breadcrumbs.

Add the yoghurt and stir it in with a large spoon until the mixture comes together in a sticky mass. Tip onto a floured surface and knead lightly to incorporate. The dough should not be over handled, so work lightly and keep the kneading to a minimum. Lightly flour a sturdy baking sheet. Flour a rolling pin and roll out the dough to a thickness of 2.5 cm/1 inch. Dip a 6 cm/2¼ inch round cutter in flour and cut out rounds of dough, Bake the scones for 10 minutes or until the bases are crisp and the tops are nicely browned. Eat hot as a breakfast accompaniment.

Buttery, creamy scrambled eggs

Serves 2
Preparation time: 5 minutes

4 large free-range eggs
30 g/1 oz butter
2 tablespoons double cream
sea salt and freshly ground black pepper

The secret of fabulously rich scrambled eggs is lots of butter and a dash of cream, although both can be reduced for a healthier, yet still tasty option.

The gentle stirring of the eggs results in a thick and creamy curd-like mass. Scrambled eggs must come off the heat when still slightly liquid as they will carry on cooking in their own heat.

Break the eggs into a bowl and whisk lightly. Place a non-stick pan over a medium heat and add the butter, swirling it around to coat the base. Pour the beaten eggs into the pan and stir gently for 1½–2 minutes or until the eggs are almost cooked through. Add the cream and seasoning and stir for a few more seconds. Take off the heat and serve immediately with hot buttered toast.

Eggs – poached, boiled and fried

Sometimes the simplest recipes are the best. The following three recipes are staples of many favourite breakfasts and can be relied upon to set you up well for the day ahead.

Poached eggs

These poached eggs will have a soft, runny yolk. Cook them a little longer if you prefer a firmer set yolk.

4 large free-range eggs, at room temperature
1 tablespoon white wine vinegar

Place a wide pan over a medium heat and add a few inches of water. Add the white wine vinegar and bring to a gentle simmer. Break an egg into a small cup and gently slide into the hot water. Repeat with 3 more eggs. Cook for 4 minutes, remove with a slotted spoon and place on absorbent kitchen paper to drain.

Soft-boiled eggs

These boiled eggs will have soft oozy yolks and just set whites. Boil them for a little longer if you prefer your yolks firmly set.

4 large free-range eggs, at room temperature

Using a tablespoon, lower the eggs, one by one, into a small pan of boiling water. Cook for 4½ minutes then remove from the water and place in egg cups.

Fried eggs

These fried eggs will have softish yolks and cooked, slightly crispy whites. If you prefer set yolks just flip the egg over and cook to your liking.

4 large free-range eggs
4 tablespoons vegetable oil

Place a large non-stick frying pan over a high heat and add the oil. Get the oil really hot, then crack in the eggs and turn the heat down to medium. Cook the eggs for 2–2½ minutes, basting the yolk and whites with the oil as it cooks. The edges should be crispy and the yolks will be runny but set around the edges. Remove with a spatula and serve.

Index

First published in 2005 by Conran Octopus Limited,
a part of Octopus Publishing Group,
2–4 Heron Quays, London E14 4JP
www.conran-octopus.co.uk

Publishing Director: Lorraine Dickey
Commissioning Editor: Katey Day
Art Director: Chi Lam
Design: Carl Hodson
Photography: Tara Fisher
Prop Stylist: Chloe Brown
Production Manager: Angela Couchman
Home Economy: Jacque Malouf

British Cataloguing-in-Publication Data.
A catalogue record for this book is available
from the British Library

ISBN 1 84091 414 9

To order please ring Conran Octopus Direct
on 01903 828503

Printed and bound in China

Author's Acknowledgements

Thank you...
Katey for being a very cool editor
Tara for taking beautiful photos
Carl for your creative book design
Harry for being a generous assistant – thanks for the polenta
    cake recipe
Chloe for sourcing perfect props
KitchenAid and Neff for making recipe testing a joy
Mike Wood at Personal Catering for supplying the best fruit
Catherine Tough for the adorable little woolly egg hats
Joe McDermott at La Galette for galette making tips

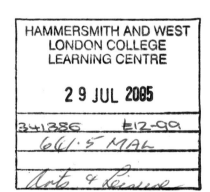